# REACHING NEW HEIGHTS

GOD'S ANSWERS TO YOUNG TEENS' QUESTIONS

VOLUME 1: JANUARY–MARCH

I0152996

## DON MEINBERG

## LUCIDBOOKS

**Reaching New Heights**
God's Answers to Young Teens' Questions
Volume 1: January–March

Copyright © 2018 by Don Meinberg

Published by Lucid Books in Houston, TX
www.LucidBooksPublishing.com

All verses marked with an asterisk (*) are the author's own paraphrase.

ISBN-10: 1-63296-247-0
ISBN-13: 978-1-63296-247-8
eISBN-10: 1-63296-249-7
eISBN-13: 978-63296-249-2

# TABLE OF CONTENTS

"I have known Pastor Don Meinberg for over 7 years, since the time he planted Reflections Christian Fellowship in Southern California. During that time, I have seen his energy and enthusiasm, not only for God but also for kids. I have read his *Reaching New Heights* series and believe that they are great books for young people going through the tough pre-teen and teenage years. The daily topics are what middle school and young high school kids may experience for the first time, and his format will definitely help kids learn how to use the Bible to deal with problems. These books are needed, especially in today's world."

**—Jeff Ludington,**
Lead Pastor at Generations Church;
author of *Frustrated: How the Bible Resolves Life's Tough Questions*

"I have known Pastor Don for over 25 years. He has a true love for Jesus and especially for kids. He has worked many years with middle school and high school kids in building them up in the Lord. His book series *Reaching New Heights* is a must-read for any young person going through the difficult years of puberty and beyond. It is a unique book series that gives kids God-centered advice on some difficult topics that they might be experiencing for the first time. Every middle school and young high school student needs this book series to help them answer the tough questions of life in a Christ-centered way. It will bless kids and parents alike!"

**—Mark Bridgeford,**
Elder, Summit Ridge Church, Rancho Cucamonga, California

"*Reaching New Heights* would be a valuable resource for any pastor, youth worker, or parent's library. As adolescent young brains are developing, they need time to think through the issues of their lives and experience God speaking directly to them in His word. These amazing books provide such a great resource and would bless the lives and homes of Christians with clarity and substance. Best of all, I can see this series being the catalyst for opening lines of communication and dialogue within families and churches. It is highly recommended."

**—Tommy Peterson,**
Youth Pastor, Bethel Baptist Church

"As a fifteen-year-old girl, I find that these books fit right in with the things that happen in school and church all the time. It helps to read what the Bible tells us to do in all these situations and to see the solutions to these difficult issues of life. *Reaching New Heights* contains a wide range of topics and hits the specific audience where things are very relative. It provides Scripture for different learning types and is well-laid-out for each question and answer."

**—Tori Hitchcock,**
Escondido, California

# INTRODUCTION

The purpose of this book is to give kids in middle school to high school between the ages of 10 and 15 a place to find God's answers for problems they face daily. There are numerous books and other publications that focus only on high school or college age kids and the struggles and problems they face regarding drugs and alcohol, dating, sex, jobs, and career choices. But my research found that very few books concentrate solely on questions that young teens or preteens face in their everyday lives. Their issues may be similar to the topics facing high school and college age kids but from a totally different perspective. Younger kids may be facing some of these issues for the very first time and are confused and frustrated. Also, their questions are more likely to be about lying to elders, cheating on tests, new friendships, temptations, and difficult choices. This book gives them an avenue to learn what God says about these issues and how to apply God's answers to their lives in a language they can understand.

The book is formatted with an advice-column look with the main topic at the top of the page and the related issue or question directly below. The issues or questions are mainly presented as stories that young teens might be experiencing. But the beauty of this book is that young teens or preteens can revise the story content to fit a similar problem or issue they are encountering that is related to the main topic. They can do that for any of the main topics in the book.

Following each question or issue is a section called "What God Says." It includes the book, chapter, and verse in the Bible that directly relates to the question and main topic. Sometimes, a paraphrase of the verse is used.

It may or may not include the entire verse, depending on the issue. I paraphrase some verses to make it easier for the reader to understand and apply the appropriate meaning of the verse to the subject or question. The Bible translation used in this book is the New Living Translation, chosen for its accuracy and its easy-to-read format.

Below the Bible's solution to the issue is the application of God's answer. Sometimes, it is extremely difficult to interpret what the Bible means and apply it to the problem at hand. This section does that for the reader, breaking down God's words into practical terms that young teens can understand and use to solve their own dilemmas. Each answer is unique to the question presented and God's solution to that issue.

Once the young teen has read the issue, learned God's solution, and understood its meaning by applying the verse, they are ready for the next section called "Questions to Ponder." Here, we want our young students to write down their thoughts and notes on what they just read. Each topic includes a couple of questions to guide them along in their thinking. This section is a tool that can be used for open discussion among a group of young teens, or it can be used as a tool for individuals to write down their own thoughts and ideas and how they apply to their own situation.

At the top of each journal page is a motto that directly relates to the main topic. The purpose of the motto is to give the reader one final thought on the main topic and hopefully inspire them to remember this topic and solution for a long time. The young teen may not remember the story or the Bible verse, but chances are good that they will remember the motto because it is only one line directed exclusively at the main topic.

There are very few (if any) books available for young teens and preteens ages 10 to 15 that relate directly to them and their needs from a biblical perspective. It takes those difficult issues—prayers not answered, lack of communication with parents—for young teens to understand and apply God's word. This is a book for their level of maturity written primarily for their age group, focusing totally on questions and problems in their lives with useful God-inspired answers. This book will teach young teens right from wrong with a biblical stance on tough issues that would make even adults cringe. This book could become a source of enlightenment for students and an answered prayer for the adults in their lives.

This book can be used in a variety of ways: as a daily devotional for a year, as an advice textbook, as a diary of solutions to teens' problems, or as a memorable book of stories with God's solutions.

## LOSING A FRIEND

**Q:** I have a best friend whom I've known for many years. We have been best friends, almost inseparable. But last month, she started to change. She started to hang out with other kids and dress way different than before. Then my "best friend" did the ultimate worst thing to me. We had shared many secrets about things such as our dreams, our future boyfriend types, and other girl stuff. She started telling these secrets to those other kids, laughing with them at me about what a baby I am. I was so angry, I cried for a week. I thought I could trust her with my intimate thoughts, but she is a backstabber. I don't know if I'll ever be able to trust a friend again.

> **What God Says**: Psalm 55:22 *"Give your burdens to the LORD, and He will take care of you. He will not permit the godly to slip and fall."*

**A:** It must have been devastating for you to have your best friend turn on you like that. What in the world was she thinking? You may think today that you'll never be able to trust your friend again, but there are ways to change that thought. One thing we must always remember is that God is our constant friend, and He promises that He will never leave us or fail us. Talk to God, and ask Him to give you strength and wisdom to find other friends who won't betray you. Sometimes, the lessons of life are extremely difficult, but it's nice to know that you have a father in heaven who will always be there in your time of need.

### Questions to ponder:
Have you ever had a friend stab you in the back?

If so, how did you handle it?

If not, how would you handle it?

God will never leave you.

**JOURNAL:**

# ATTITUDE

**Q:** I hate doing chores at home. To me, it's like I have better things to do than work around the house. It seems like none of my other friends have to do as many chores as I do. So when my dad gives me a list of chores to do, like clean my room or take out the trash or wash the car, I can't help but get a really bad attitude by rolling my eyes or saying something mean under my breath. My dad knows I'd rather be skating with my friends or riding my bike, but he constantly gives me these dumb chores. And it seems like the more attitude I give him, the more chores he makes me do. So I look like I enjoy doing these silly tasks, but in reality, I have a terrible attitude against him.

**What God Says:** Ephesians 6:6–7 *Work hard but not just to please your master when they are watching. As slaves of Christ, do the will of God with all your heart. Work with enthusiasm as though you were working for the Lord rather than for people.*\*

**A:** I don't think there are many kids anywhere who love to do chores. I'm sure there are many parents who don't like to work around the house, either. I'm sure your mom doesn't jump up and down with joy to wash your dirty socks and underwear. We need to work with enthusiasm at anything we do for whoever needs help. We need to keep in mind that we are serving God as well as people and that He will bless us if we perform our duties with a cheerful attitude. All things in life are good or bad based on what attitude we take. Do as God instructs, and be a happier person.

## Questions to ponder:

What type of thing gives you attitude?

How do you manage it?

Work for God with a cheerful heart.

**JOURNAL:** _____

_____

_____

_____

_____

_____

_____

_____

_____

_____

_____

_____

_____

_____

_____

_____

_____

_____

_____

_____

_____

_____

## SELF-CONTROL

**Q:** I have a problem with my big mouth at home. Whenever I get in an argument with my mom or even my brother, I start getting real sassy and mouthy, and I can't seem to control it. Then, my mouth usually gets me in more trouble. I have really put an effort into controlling my temper, but when things don't go the way I want, I just can't control myself. Now, I'm starting to lose control of my mouth at school and with my friends. I really need to get my anger and my big mouth under control, but I don't know how. It seems like everyone hates me, and it's all my fault.

**What God Says**: Proverbs 13:3 *Those who control the tongue will have a long life; a quick retort can ruin everything.**

**A:** There is a great way to learn the basics of self-control: Never say the first thing that pops into your head. The normal response when we are angry is to say something insulting or mean or something we will probably regret. Pausing a few seconds and thinking prior to speaking will allow you to calm down a bit and breathe more relaxed. That will help you think with a clear, relaxed mind. God teaches us that a quick response (without thinking) will ruin everything. Another thing that helps is talking to God before reacting. It definitely helps reduce the adrenaline and keep you in control.

**Questions to ponder:**

What gets out of control in your life?

How do you put it back in control?

Let God control your temper.

**JOURNAL:** _____

_____

_____

_____

_____

_____

_____

_____

_____

_____

_____

_____

_____

_____

_____

_____

_____

_____

_____

_____

_____

_____

_____

_____

_____

## DEALING WITH IMPATIENT KIDS

**Q:** My friend has a puppy that she loves dearly. She's had this puppy for about a year, and she totally takes care of it. This dog stays in the house most of the time, but the other day, the puppy saw a cat outside and darted out the open door. My friend thought the puppy would return right away, but she didn't. Since that time, she has been praying to God to bring her puppy back to her, but so far, the dog has not returned. She told me yesterday that she has no more patience with God and that her puppy is lost forever. I told her not to quit praying and that God was listening. She told me she has given up on God and that waiting for Him is a waste of time.

> **What God Says:** Romans 8:25 "But *if we look forward to something we don't yet have, we must wait patiently and confidently.*"

**A:** It sure seems that your friend's faith in God is low if she gives up and has no patience for Him that quickly. Patience is produced by having total faith in God and allowing Him to do the work in your life. God hears all prayers and listens to our needs. We need to tell impatient kids that God loves them and will answer their prayers in His perfect timing. That may mean your friend's puppy is lost forever, but something better may come along later—maybe something your friend doesn't expect. Always have patience and faith in your father in heaven.

**Question to ponder:**

What has happened in your life that made you lose patience with God? Explain.

God always has perfect timing.

**JOURNAL:**

11

# JANUARY 5

**Q:** In my neighborhood, there is a group of kids who hang out together. About two weeks ago, I started hanging out with them. It seemed like all these kids ever did was either insult every kid who passed by, throw mud at cars, or start fights with kids from another block. They thought all that was funny. I didn't participate in any of these activities at first, but after a while, I noticed that my behavior was starting to change. Before, I was never a mean or insensitive kid. But lately, I've started to join in the verbal abuse and the mud throwing and even dressing like them. I'm now considered one of them, but I'm not sure that's what I want to be.

> **What God Says**: 1 Thessalonians 1:7 *As a result, you yourselves became an example to all the Christians in Greece.**

**A:** It's like the old saying: "A bad tree will yield bad fruit." If something looks like a frog, jumps like a frog, and acts like a frog, then it's probably a frog. It is the same with that group of neighborhood kids. If the group talks like troublemakers, acts like troublemakers, and dresses like troublemakers, they probably are troublemakers. God wants us to be model kids in our neighborhoods, standing for everything good and right. If the kids you hang out with are not model kids, then God says to run the other way as fast as you can and not associate with evil. We have the perfect example to live by in the person of Jesus Christ.

## Question to ponder:

How do you handle a bad influence in your life?
Give a specific example.

A good tree will yield good fruit.

**JOURNAL:** _____

_____
_____
_____
_____
_____
_____
_____
_____
_____
_____
_____
_____
_____
_____
_____
_____
_____
_____
_____
_____
_____

# DEALING WITH DISRESPECTFUL KIDS

**Q:** There is a kid in my class who is totally disrespectful to the teachers and the aides. When the teacher is trying to teach the class, he is always disruptive, talking to others, passing notes, or laughing out loud. When the teachers ask him to be quiet, he is extremely sassy, saying mean things, or he just ignores them. He has been disciplined many times, but it doesn't seem to change him. Even when some of the parents come to help in the classroom, he's very mean and disrespectful to them. He's arrogant and loud, and we're really getting tired of it.

> <u>**What God Says**</u>: I Peter 5:5 *You younger men, accept the authority of the elders. And all of you serve each other in humility. God sets Himself against the proud, but He shows favor to the humble.*\*

**A:** When a kid acts loud and obnoxious, it is very difficult to try to teach him about humility. Being totally disrespectful to teachers, aides, and parents shows the pride this kid has in himself, setting himself up as a tough guy. God does not care about tough guys; as a matter of fact, He dishonors them. That is because God is about love, honor, and respect for others. The best way to handle this kid is to ignore his antics and continue to respect your elders with humility as God teaches. If this kid realizes he's not getting the attention he wants, he may stop his arrogant and disrespectful ways.

## Questions to ponder:

Are you sometimes disrespectful to your elders?

What causes you to be disrespectful?

How can you change your disrespectful attitude?

Always respect your elders.

**JOURNAL:** _____

_____
_____
_____
_____
_____
_____
_____
_____
_____
_____
_____
_____
_____
_____
_____
_____
_____
_____
_____
_____
_____
_____

# PEER PRESSURE

**Q:** I have a core of about four friends I mostly hang out with every day at school. We all have the same classes together, and we usually sit by each other. Now, I've always been a good student. I usually get straight As, but my friends have always struggled in school, and they usually get Cs or Ds on their tests. The other day, we had a midterm exam in history, and they told me that the only way they would pass was if I let them see my answers. Because they were my friends, I did it. Tomorrow, we have an important English test, and they are putting a lot of pressure on me to do it again. I don't like people to cheat, and I surely don't want to get caught, but I also don't want to lose my friends.

---

**What God Says**: 1 Corinthians 15:33 *"Don't be fooled by those who say such things, for 'bad company corrupts good character.'"*

---

**A:** God tells us that our character and our integrity are extremely important, and we should not allow anyone to destroy them. If kids are leading you to evil, then they are not your true friends. If you allow them to cheat on this English test, then when will it ever end? The next test after that, they will want the same thing. It needs to stop now. Instead, you should offer to tutor them or study with them, so they can learn the material. If these kids will not be your friends or put a lot of pressure on you because you won't help them to cheat, then they were never your friends to begin with. They are only using you. You need to get different friends who share your godly values.

## Question to ponder:

How do you handle peer pressure in your life?
Give specific examples.

Don't let peer pressure destroy
your good character.

**JOURNAL:**

## HELPING A SINNER GROW

**Q:** I have a friend at school who is a really nice person with a good heart. The problem is that she struggles mightily with sin. Now, I know we all sin, but she is either lying to her parents, cheating at school, stealing petty things at a store, or being mean to kids in her neighborhood all the time. She says she does most of these sinful acts for the right reasons. She lied to her parents to help a friend not get busted for drugs. She cheated at school by giving her friend answers on a test because her friend didn't have a chance to study. She stole candy at a store to give it to a boy who was hungry, and she was mean to other kids who were being mean to her sister. Her heart is in the right place, but her behavior is wrong. She knows what she is doing is wrong, but she doesn't know how to change.

**What God Says**: Colossians 2:14 *He canceled the record that contained the charges against us. He took it and destroyed it by nailing it to Christ's cross.**

**A:** So, your friend has good intentions but bad execution. Her heart might be in the right place, but her behavior needs a little tweaking. To change sinful behavior, the person needs to turn to God and ask Him for forgiveness from the heart. Then, the person needs to pray for wisdom to continue to do the right thing but in the right way. God welcomes all sinners who actively seek Him with a sincere heart. Christ's death on the cross gave sinners like us a chance for new life if we ask for it.

**Questions to ponder:**

Do you have a friend who constantly sins?

How do you help them change their ways?

Trust God to help you change
from your sinful ways.

**JOURNAL:**_____

_____

_____

_____

_____

_____

_____

_____

_____

_____

_____

_____

_____

_____

_____

_____

_____

_____

_____

_____

_____

_____

_____

## MODESTY

**Q:** I am a 12-year-old girl, and I want to dress any way I like. I enjoy wearing really tight jeans or spaghetti strap tops to school or the mall and watching all the guys just drool over me. It is fun when I wear a short dress or miniskirt and watch the boys try to get close to me. My parents give me a real tough time, telling me that I dress way too sexy or provocative and that I could get hurt in the long run. I love all the attention I get from boys, especially when they go out of their way to flirt with me. Since it is my body and I'm not hurting anyone, I don't understand why I can't dress the way I want without getting hassled by my parents.

**What God Says**: 1 Timothy 2:9 *"I want women to be modest in their appearance. They should wear decent and appropriate clothing and not draw attention to themselves."*

**A:** The type of attention you describe is not good for the soul. In today's world, it is extremely dangerous to dress in revealing, sexy clothes because the consequences far exceed any advantage of extra attention. God is very straightforward that inward beauty that attracts attention is much more important than outward appearance from wearing inappropriate clothing. The type of attention you're getting is the kind you really don't want. Guys may take advantage of you, or you could get a reputation for being "easy." Be modest in your appearance, and allow your inward beauty to shine.

### Questions to ponder:

Do you agree that girls and guys should be modest in what they wear? Why or why not?

Be modest, and people will respect you more.

**JOURNAL:** _____

_____

_____

_____

_____

_____

_____

_____

_____

_____

_____

_____

_____

_____

_____

_____

_____

_____

_____

_____

_____

_____

# DEALING WITH VAIN KIDS

**Q:** Have you ever had a friend who could not go five minutes without looking at himself or herself in the mirror? That perfectly describes one of my friends at school. Her best friend is her mirror, and she goes nowhere without it. She is only 14 years old, and yet she is always checking her makeup and her hair to make sure she looks perfect. She's a good friend, but this obsession with her outer appearance is really getting on my nerves. You should see her bedroom. She has a mirror on every wall, so no matter where she looks, she can see herself. I wish she would concentrate her attention more on our friendship and less on herself.

> **What God Says**: Proverbs 31:30 *"Charm is deceptive, and beauty does not last; but a woman who fears the LORD will be greatly praised."*

**A:** You need to tell your friend that outward beauty reveals only what we look like, but inner beauty reveals who we are. Loving others and helping those in need should be your best friends, not the mirror. God could care less what you look like on the outside; it's what you have on the inside that counts. Your friendship and your friend's relationship with God are so much more important than her outer appearance. You need to tell her that she must build on something that will last throughout eternity, not on something that will eventually fade away.

### Questions to ponder:

What do you think of kids who are vain and snooty?

Do you know someone like that? Explain.

Inward beauty is more important
than outward appearance.

**JOURNAL:** _____

_____

_____

_____

_____

_____

_____

_____

_____

_____

_____

_____

_____

_____

_____

_____

_____

_____

_____

_____

_____

_____

_____

_____

_____

_____

_____

## GOD'S WILL

**Q:** I'm a baseball fanatic. I love to play baseball and watch baseball on television. There isn't much about baseball that I don't know, including the rules, the players on every team, and even the main statistics of the best players. The problem is that I'm not very good at playing baseball. I can catch the ball, but I can't hit very well. On the other hand, I play the tuba very well, good enough to beat out six other kids for the middle school band. But I can't stand lugging around this large, heavy instrument everywhere I go, and I certainly don't enjoy it as much as baseball, but I know I can't do both. I want to know which one God would want me to do.

**What God Says**: Psalm 32:8 *"The LORD says, 'I will guide you along the best pathway for your life. I will advise you and watch over you.'"*

**A:** We need to trust God and ask Him what He wants us to do in our lives. He will answer us either through His word, through people, or through circumstances (not making the baseball team). He alone knows the best path for our lives, so if we pray to Him, He will guide us in the right direction. Once you decide to allow God to guide you down the right path, you need to trust Him completely, even if the path is not necessarily the one you wanted. Take God's advice, and you know you'll always be going down the right road.

## Questions to ponder:
What do you think is God's will in your life?

How do you know?

Let God's will be done in your life.

**JOURNAL:**

_____

_____

_____

_____

_____

_____

_____

_____

_____

_____

_____

_____

_____

_____

_____

_____

_____

_____

_____

_____

_____

_____

# JANUARY 12

## DEALING WITH SELFISH KIDS

**Q:** There is a kid in my class who is always bragging about all the things she has and all the money her family has. She is probably wealthier than most kids and has all the cool technological gadgets at her house. The problem is that she wouldn't share even a pencil with anyone in the class. She is extremely selfish, and we all know that she has enough "stuff" to give to other less fortunate kids, but she refuses to share. Except for that, she's a pretty nice kid, but it really bugs me how someone could be so selfish. Is there a way I could possibly get her to share?

> **What God Says**: Philippians 2:3 *Don't be selfish; don't live to make a good impression on others. Be humble, thinking of others as better than yourself.*\*

**A:** It is extremely difficult to teach someone humility or a sharing heart. All you can do is teach by example. You need to continue to think of the well-being of others more than yourself and be tenderhearted toward others in your class. Maybe, when she sees how blessed you are by your actions, she'll start to mend her ways and not be as selfish. Read the verse above again and notice that God teaches us to be humble in everything we do, thinking of others ahead of ourselves.

## Questions to ponder:

Do you know selfish kids?

How do you deal with them?

God loves an unselfish heart.

**JOURNAL:** _____

_____

_____

_____

_____

_____

_____

_____

_____

_____

_____

_____

_____

_____

_____

_____

_____

_____

_____

_____

_____

_____

## HEAVEN

**Q:** My parents are always talking to me about heaven. They tell me it's like living in the most perfect place with angels all around and God sitting on His throne with trumpets blasting. But how do I know that heaven actually exists? Like I said, the Bible says it exists, my mom and dad say it exists, and my Sunday school teacher says it exists, but how do I know for sure? Unfortunately, I am the type of person who needs to see something or feel it before I believe it. When I die, I know I go in a box in the ground forever, so how do I go from the ground to heaven? It's really confusing!

---

**What God Says**: 2 Corinthians 5:1 *For we know that when this earthly tent we live in is taken down when we die and leave these bodies, we will have a home in heaven.**

---

**A:** The way we know how to get to heaven is that God tells us in the Bible. If you read the verse above, it clearly states that when we die, we will leave these earthly bodies and be in heaven. So, you know heaven exists because God says so. You say you need to see or feel something before you believe. That's not the way it works with God. He wants us to have faith in Him, in Jesus Christ, and in heaven without seeing so that He knows our hearts. When you die, your body goes in the ground, but your soul goes straight to heaven if you lived your life for Jesus. Your body is only temporary, but your soul is eternal.

### Questions to ponder:
Do you believe heaven exists?
How do you know?

> Heaven waits for those who know Christ.

**JOURNAL:** _____

_____

_____

_____

_____

_____

_____

_____

_____

_____

_____

_____

_____

_____

_____

_____

_____

_____

_____

_____

_____

_____

_____

## HELPING A SCARED FRIEND

**Q:** My friend has not seen her dad since she was a baby. He left town when she was three months old, and now she's 13. She has been trying for the last couple of years to find him so she can see what he's like. Somehow, her teacher used the Internet to locate him, and they made arrangements to have him come to my friend's house tomorrow night. Right now, she is scared to death. She is worried that he might not like her or that she's not what he expected or that he will leave her again. Her mom will be with her, but she still has quite a few emotions and is scared that the reunion will not go well. What is the best way to comfort her?

**What God Says**: Deuteronomy 20:3 *He will say, "Listen to me all you men of Israel. Do not be afraid. Do not lose heart or panic."*

**A:** No matter what the situation—facing impossible odds of achieving something or being involved in an uncomfortable situation like seeing a long-lost dad—God is always able to bring peace and strength to all who ask Him for it. Tell your friend to pray to God and tell Him her fears and anxieties, and let His mighty hand comfort her. He does not want us to be afraid or lose heart or panic when facing our fears. He wants to guide us with peace and love. God will make all things right for those who trust in Him.

**Question to ponder:**

How do you help a scared friend?
Explain in detail.

Turn first to God in times of fear.

**JOURNAL:** _____

_____

_____

_____

_____

_____

_____

_____

_____

_____

_____

_____

_____

_____

_____

_____

_____

_____

_____

_____

_____

_____

# JANUARY 15

## SUFFERING

**Q:** I am a believer in Jesus Christ as my Lord and savior, and all my faith is in Him. But I get teased and ridiculed by my non-Christian classmates for it. I get called names like "goody-two-shoes," "Jesus freak," and other names that make me feel really bad. It seems like the only times I don't get teased is when I'm in church. Because of this, I suffer every day by being lonely and hurt. Sometimes, it gets to the point that I want to tell these kids that I quit going to church so the suffering will stop. If God loves me, then why do I have to suffer so much because I believe in Him? Why can't God take away the pain and suffering I feel?

> **What God Says**: Romans 8:17–18 *Since we are His children, we will share in His treasures—for everything God gives to His son is ours, too. But if we are to share in His glory, we are also to share in is suffering. Yet what we suffer now is nothing compared to the glory He will give us later.*\*

**A:** We need to keep in mind that any suffering we experience for our faith is pleasing to God. To share in God's glory means to share in God's suffering. But the reward in heaven makes it all worthwhile. Also, remember that Jesus suffered during His time here on earth. He endured ridicule, mocking, and physical abuse just to save us from our sins. Jesus suffered torture and death on the cross for us. So if you are suffering for God's sake, you are in great company. Talk to God and ask Him for strength in your faith, and your rewards in heaven will be great.

### Questions to ponder:
Have you ever suffered for your love of God?

If yes, how did you handle it?

If no, how would you handle it?

> Jesus says blessed are those
> persecuted for my sake.

**JOURNAL:**

_____

_____

_____

_____

_____

_____

_____

_____

_____

_____

_____

_____

_____

_____

_____

_____

_____

_____

_____

_____

_____

## DEALING WITH UNRELIABLE FRIENDS

**Q:** I have a good friend who is extremely unreliable. Any time she says she'll do something for me or promises to deliver a message for me, she forgets to do it. For example, the other day I couldn't make it to band practice because I had a doctor's appointment for my allergies. I asked her to tell my band teacher that I had an excused absence. Well, my friend completely forgot to tell my teacher, and I got marked down for an unexcused absence. When I help her with her homework, I can't rely on her to give my notes back to me. When I let her borrow things, she loses them. I love her a lot as a friend, but I don't know how I can start trusting her with anything.

> **What God Says**: 1 John 4:16 *We know how much God loves us, and we have put our trust in Him.*\*

**A:** It's very difficult when a good friend is unreliable. Putting your faith in someone is a big step for most of us, and when that faith is broken time and time again, it becomes very disheartening. You need to talk to your friend about God and her problem and then have her ask Him for help in becoming more reliable. That way, you can start trusting her again, but only with small, insignificant things. When she proves to be reliable with the small things, give her more substantial things as she grows in Christ. But remember to start with prayer first, and always put your trust in God.

### Questions to ponder:

Do you have unreliable friends?

How do you help them become more reliable?

God can make an unreliable soul truly reliable.

**JOURNAL:**_____

_____

_____

_____

_____

_____

_____

_____

_____

_____

_____

_____

_____

_____

_____

_____

_____

_____

_____

_____

_____

# JANUARY 17

## ANGER

**Q:** It seem like I'm always angry at my stepmom. She really does try hard not to act like she's my real mom, but whenever she disciplines me or asks me to do anything, I get very angry and say things I shouldn't say. I guess I was very bitter when my mom and dad separated. I loved being a family, and when all of a sudden they decided to divorce, it made me extremely angry inside. I think I take some of that anger out on my new stepmom. I actually do like her, but she's not my real mom, and I just can't get over that. Still, I need to give her more of a chance and not lash out at her in anger. What do you suggest so I can control my tongue?

> **What God Says**: James 3:5 *The tongue is a small thing, but what enormous damage it can do.**

**A:** Your stepmom is a human being and a child of God and should be treated with love and respect, just like you would treat any other person. It is not fair for you to treat your stepmom so rudely because of a situation that has little to do with her. Read James 3:5 again. Your tongue can cause tremendous damage when used without thinking. Try to avoid speaking your mind when you are angry. You will, more times than not, say something you will regret later. Instead of getting angry and saying something mean, say a quick prayer to God to give you wisdom before you speak.

## Questions to ponder:

Is there someone in your life that makes you angry a lot?

How do you handle your anger?

God says to think before you talk.

**JOURNAL:** _____

_____

_____

_____

_____

_____

_____

_____

_____

_____

_____

_____

_____

_____

_____

_____

_____

_____

_____

_____

_____

_____

# JANUARY 18

## NEVER SATISFIED

**Q:** I'm 13 years old, a straight A student, captain of my tennis team, and very popular at school. I'm pretty good at most things, and my life seems to be going well. The problem is that I'm extremely hard on myself, and I am never satisfied with my accomplishments. I get real angry at myself when I get a B on a test or if I lose a tennis match. I'm always striving to be better at everything, and when I do better, I'm reaching for the next goal instead of being satisfied with accomplishing the last goal. People around me are always saying how smart and talented I am, but I have a hard time believing it.

> **What God Says**: Psalm 63:5 *You satisfy me more than the richest of foods. I will praise you with songs of joy.**

**A:** We must remember that our beauty, our intelligence, our talents, and all our accomplishments are gifts from God. He is the one who gives us all these things so we can use them in honor of Him. Believing in God and living by His word should satisfy you to the fullest as the verse above says. Satisfaction comes from within, and when we realize who the true owner of these gifts is, we are better able to cope with our achievements.

### Questions to ponder:
Do you know people who are never satisfied?
What's your opinion of these people?

God satisfies all our needs.

**JOURNAL:** _____

_____

_____

_____

_____

_____

_____

_____

_____

_____

_____

_____

_____

_____

_____

_____

_____

_____

_____

_____

_____

_____

# JANUARY 19

## BLAMING

**Q:** It seems like I'm always getting blamed for things my younger brother does. If we are playing outside and we *both* do something we know is wrong, I will get the blame, and my younger brother doesn't get into any trouble at all. My parents say that because I am older, I should know better. But my brother is only two years younger than I am, so why is everything always my fault? Here's an example: We were playing baseball in our front yard. I threw a pitch, and my brother hit the ball through a window. When we told our parents what happened, I got in trouble for playing too close to the house, and yet he was the one who hit the ball through the window. So now when I'm with my younger brother, he knows he won't be blamed when something goes wrong, and I will.

**What God Says**: 1 Thessalonians 3:13 *Christ will make your heart strong, blameless, and holy when you stand before God our father on that day when our Lord Jesus comes with all those who belong to Him.*\*

**A:** Your mom and dad may not have all the facts when you and your brother do something wrong, but God does. It may be frustrating for you as the older brother to be blamed for everything, but the good thing is that if we live our lives for Jesus and believe in Him, our sins (or wrongs) are forgiven, and we will be blameless in the eyes of the Lord almighty. So I wouldn't worry too much about being blamed for your brother's mistakes. Just put your faith in Christ, ask Him for help, and you'll be fine.

## Question to ponder:

What do you do when you are wrongfully blamed?
Give specific examples.

When you are wrongfully blamed, seek God.

**JOURNAL:**

_____

_____

_____

_____

_____

_____

_____

_____

_____

_____

_____

_____

_____

_____

_____

_____

_____

_____

_____

_____

_____

_____

## HELL

**Q:** I have a lot of questions about hell. There are things about it that just don't make a lot of sense to me. First of all, does hell really exist? Since God is all about love, then how could He send good people to hell? All I read about in the Bible and hear from my parents and Sunday school teachers is that God is loving, kind, merciful, and full of grace. How can a God who is that wonderful send people to hell? I know I want to spend eternity with God in heaven, but I have a hard time believing that good people go to hell. How do I make sure I don't go to hell?

> **What God Says**: Matthew 13:49–50 *That is the way it will be at the end of the world. The angels will come and separate the wicked people from the godly, throwing the wicked in the fire.*\*

**A:** First of all, yes, hell really does exist. We know that because God tells us so in the Bible. Read the passage above. When God says He will throw the wicked in the fire, those are the people going to hell. Remember, God gives us all a choice to either follow Him or not, and the choice we make determines where we will spend eternity. God does not send people to hell. People send themselves to hell by not believing in His word. You can make sure you don't go to hell by believing in Christ as your savior and living your life for God.

### Questions to ponder:

Do you believe hell exists?

How do you know for sure?

God has a place in heaven
for those who follow Him.

**JOURNAL:**

# EMBARRASSMENT

**Q:** Most of the kids I hang out with either at school or around the neighborhood are non-Christians. I go to church every Sunday and youth group every Tuesday night. My friends are always asking me to join them on Sunday mornings at the mall, on Saturday night for a sleepover, or on Tuesday after school for an activity. I sometimes get embarrassed by always saying no because I have to go to church. I sometimes get so embarrassed that I lie and tell them I have other plans. Now don't get me wrong, I love going to church and want to continue, but I love my friends and don't want to feel embarrassed anymore.

**What God Says**: 2 Timothy 1:8 *You must never be ashamed to tell others about our Lord.*\*

**A:** If your friends were good, true friends, they would definitely understand your dedication to church and youth activities. If they don't understand and make you feel embarrassed, then they were never true friends to begin with. Why can't you plan activities with them on the other days of the week or after church on Sunday? If you get out by noon, you still have the rest of the day to be with your friends. As the verse says, never be ashamed of God or His church. Don't ever compromise your faith, and always put God first in your life. Your reward in heaven will be great!

## Questions to ponder:

Have you ever been embarrassed about your love for God?

If yes, how did you handle it?

If no, how would you handle it?

Never be embarrassed about your love for God.

**JOURNAL:** _____

_____

_____

_____

_____

_____

_____

_____

_____

_____

_____

_____

_____

_____

_____

_____

_____

_____

_____

_____

_____

_____

_____

_____

# JANUARY 22

## DEALING WITH PREJUDICED PEOPLE

**Q:** I am a very good swimmer. I have been swimming since I was four years old. I tried out for the city team, but the coach would not allow me on it because I'm a Latino girl. It is a boy's swim team, but since there aren't any girls' teams in the city, it is the only opportunity I have to participate. They have had girls on the team, but they were all white. I know it's tougher for me because I'm a girl, but I'm pretty sure the coach is prejudiced against the Latin American culture. He never said it, but I can tell by his attitude and the way he treated me. What makes it worse is that my swim times are as good or better than the boys. How can I deal with such prejudice?

> **What God Says**: 2 Chronicles 19:7 *Fear the LORD and judge with care, for the LORD our God does not tolerate perverted justice, partiality, or the taking of bribes.**

**A:** God hates the sin of prejudice because He created us all the same in His image and likeness, and we are His children no matter if we are Caucasian, African American, Asian, Latino, Indian, or anything else. In God's eyes, no race or ethnic background is better than another. There is no superior gender. God would want you to stand up for your rights. You need to ask this coach why you are not allowed on the team since your times are as good as the boys' times. If he doesn't give you a good answer, go to his authority. Only God is our judge, and He shows no partiality to anyone.

## Question to ponder:

What do you think of people who are prejudiced toward others because of their ethnic background?

Give an example of someone like that.

Fight the terrible sin of prejudice.

**JOURNAL:**

## STEALING

**Q:** I'm a really big kid for my age. I'm only in the sixth grade, but I stand about 5 feet 7 inches tall and weigh over 170 pounds. I am by far the biggest kid in my class. So I take advantage of my size, and just for fun, I love taking other kids' lunch money or eating their lunches. I do it all the time, mostly to the smaller fourth- and fifth-grade kids, the ones I know can't do anything about it. These kids don't tell their teachers or their parents because they are afraid I'll pound their faces. It may not sound like it, but I'm not a bad kid. I know what I'm doing is wrong, but to me, it's a lot of fun, and I get a kick out of taking things that don't belong to me.

> **What God Says**: Ephesians 4:28 *If you are a thief, stop stealing.*＊

**A:** I'm not sure whether you are a bad kid or not. The worst kind of stealing is taking things from innocent victims who don't have a chance. If you know what you are doing is wrong, then stop doing it. God boldly states that if you are stealing from others, then stop. How much fun do you think it would be if someone over 6 feet tall weighing over 250 pounds were doing the same thing to you? The harm you do to another person is the same type of harm that will come to you. You need to turn from this sin immediately and ask God for forgiveness.

**Question to ponder:**

How can you help kids stop stealing?

Thieves are not allowed in the kingdom of God unless they repent.

**JOURNAL:** _____

_____

_____

_____

_____

_____

_____

_____

_____

_____

_____

_____

_____

_____

_____

_____

_____

_____

_____

_____

_____

_____

_____

_____

# DEALING WITH KIDS WHO WORRY

**Q:** My friend is trying out for the seventh-grade basketball team. He's a pretty good player but not as good as most of the other players trying out for the team. Most of the other kids are taller than he is and can jump higher. He has a nice shot, but he's not very quick, so his shots can be easily blocked. He really wants to make the team, and for the last couple of weeks, he's been losing sleep at night worrying about it. The more I tell him not to worry, the more he worries and—worse than that—the worse he plays. I'm not sure why it's so important for him to make this team, but it is. But his worrying is starting to affect his schoolwork and home life.

> **What God Says**: Philippians 4:6 *"Don't worry about anything; instead pray about everything."*

**A:** The only way to get rid of worry is to trust God and put everything in His hands. He teaches us in the above verse to stop worrying and start praying. God wants to ease our burden and take away the worries of life. Remember, we need to accept the things we cannot change. All we can do is give 100% effort and pray for the best. Whatever happens after that we can't control, so we need to give it to God. Always remember that worrying is a worthless emotion and will never make a situation better.

## Questions to ponder:

Do you have friends who worry about everything?

How do you help them calm their nerves?

Cast all your worries on God.

**JOURNAL:** _____

_____

_____

_____

_____

_____

_____

_____

_____

_____

_____

_____

_____

_____

_____

_____

_____

_____

_____

_____

_____

_____

_____

_____

# SHYNESS

**Q:** I'm in the eighth grade, and I am very shy. I rarely talk to anyone at school. Most of the time, I keep to myself. I'm not sure why I'm like that. I am an only child, and my parents give me a lot of attention, but when I leave the house, I get scared and shy. I wish I had a friend to talk to at school, but I am afraid to approach anyone. No one ever comes up to me because they think I'm too quiet and they'll have nothing to say. There are times when I enjoy being alone and reading my books, but sometimes I get sad watching other kids laughing, playing together, and having fun, but I'm too shy to join in. What can I do to get over this shyness?

**What God Says**: Matthew 28:20 *"I am with you always, even to the end of the age."*

**A:** Keep in mind that with God in your heart, you are never really alone. We can all take comfort in knowing that God is always with us and will always be there for us. But what you are doing is robbing yourself of a special gift God has provided for all of us, and that's the gift of fellowship. God put people in our lives to help and comfort us in times of sorrow and to celebrate with us in times of joy. You need to pray to God for the strength and courage to approach other kids and get them to know you so you can start building relationships. It may be uncomfortable for you at first, but at least you know you won't be doing it alone.

**Questions to ponder:**

How do you think kids get over their shyness?

Give an example of a shy kid you know and what you can do to help them.

God is with us always.

**JOURNAL:**

_____
_____
_____
_____
_____
_____
_____
_____
_____
_____
_____
_____
_____
_____
_____
_____
_____
_____
_____
_____
_____
_____
_____
_____
_____

# JANUARY 26

## DEALING WITH IGNORANT KIDS

**Q:** My friend and I have a science teacher who I'll call Mrs. X. Now, Mrs. X must be over 70 years old, and she talks in a low monotone voice. She runs a very tough class and is always disciplining the kids who are misbehaving. She is a very good teacher. If I ever have a problem with my science homework, she always makes time to explain it to me again and again until I get it. The problem is that my friend refuses to listen to her or learn from her because she is old and strict. She has become extremely ignorant about her attitude toward Mrs. X, and when I try to talk to her about it, she totally ignores me. She doesn't try at all to learn the material and only complains about the teacher. How can I help her get over her ignorance?

> **What God Says**: Proverbs 2:3–5 *Cry out for insight and understanding. Search for them. Then you will understand what it means to fear the LORD.*\*

**A:** We all must learn to fear the Lord. It is not like feeling scared and terrified but a fear that shows God reverence and respect. God put Mrs. X in that classroom for a reason. He wants you to learn from and listen to her knowledge and experience. All your friend is doing is showing her true ignorance toward another human being. To help cure her ignorance, have your friend pretend that it is our Lord teaching that science class in Mrs. X's body. Changing one's perspective should change one's attitude and hopefully eliminate the ignorance.

## Question to ponder:

How do you deal with ignorant kids?

Give a specific example.

Ignorance is a sin we must avoid.

**JOURNAL:** _____

_____
_____
_____
_____
_____
_____
_____
_____
_____
_____
_____
_____
_____
_____
_____
_____
_____
_____
_____
_____
_____
_____
_____
_____
_____

## BELONGING

**Q:** I am in the sixth grade, and I badly want to belong to a popular group in my class. It's a group of about five kids that everyone in the sixth grade looks up to and admires. Most of those kids are kind of rough. They talk mean to other kids, they sass teachers, they don't care about their grades, and they walk around like tough guys who scare most kids. I want to belong to that group because all the kids respect them, and they are so cool. They told me I had to go through some sort of initiation process to be a part of the group. I'm really not sure what that is, but it doesn't really matter, because I will do just about anything to belong.

**What God Says:** Galatians 5:24 *"Those who belong to Christ Jesus have nailed the passions and desires of their sinful nature to His cross and crucified them there."*

**A:** Why in the world would you want to belong to a group like that? It sounds like a group led by the devil to entice young kids like you to join its forces. There is nothing cool about hurting others. Being part of God's group may not be the most popular thing to do, but undoubtedly it is the most rewarding. And here is the beauty of it—there is no initiation process. Just accept Jesus as your personal Lord and savior, live your life for Him, and YOU'RE IN! What may seem like the cool group at the beginning may result in a cold, miserable ending.

## Questions to ponder:

Is there a group or club that you really want to belong to?

If so, why?

If not, why do you think kids need to belong?

Belong to the right group:
Followers of Jesus Christ.

**JOURNAL:**

# DEALING WITH KIDS WHO HATE

**Q:** A kid in my class hates a friend of mine because he's different. When I say different, I don't mean race, religion, or sexual preference. My friend is nice and smart, and most kids at my school like him. He treats everyone kindly and has a big heart. The other kid thinks my friend is a jerk and a nerd because he is nice to girls. We are at an age that boys still don't like girls that much, but my friend gave a girl a Valentine's Day card. This other jerk was so enraged and full of hate that he went and punched my friend hard in the arm for no reason. He's always telling my friend he hates him, and he insults my friend with many names. How can anyone deal with someone who hates for no reason?

> **What God Says**: John 13:34–35 *I am giving you a new commandment: Love each other. As I have loved you, you should love one another. Your love for one another will prove to the world that you are my disciples.**

**A:** God is all about love, and He loves each and every one of us very much. God doesn't know hate for His people, and He wants to change those hearts that do hate. The only way to teach a kid like this is to continue to show love and kindness. You see, when you continue to love, you draw more people to yourself and have more friends. Your friend seems like a kid who has love in his heart. This other kid needs to get the hint that his hate is not having any effect and that love will conquer hate every time. Remember, many hated Jesus, but all He showed was love.

## Questions to ponder:

Why do kids hate?

How can that hate be changed to love?

God is love. There is no room
in a person's heart for hate.

**JOURNAL:**

_____

_____

_____

_____

_____

_____

_____

_____

_____

_____

_____

_____

_____

_____

_____

_____

_____

_____

_____

# TEMPTATION

**Q:** My friends and I are all 11 years old. However, one of my friends is pretty big and could easily pass for a 15- or 16-year-old. All four of us wanted to see the new *Star Trek* movie, but it was rated PG-13. We all decided we were going to see the movie and tell our parents we went to the mall. My parents as well as my buddy's parents hate science fiction movies, so we knew they would never take us. My mom would be upset if she knew I went to a PG-13 movie without an adult or without prior permission. After the movie, I was extremely tempted to lie to my parents like the other kids and say I went to the mall. I definitely did not want to hear a lecture or, worse, get grounded.

> **What God Says**: 1 Corinthians 10:13 *Remember that the temptations that come into your life are no different from what others experience. And God is faithful. He will keep the temptation from becoming so strong that you can't stand up to it. When you are tempted, He will show you the way so that you will not give in to it.*\*

**A:** The easiest way to start moving away from God is to start giving in to temptation. The devil is always in a position to tempt us. He wants us to yield to temptation so we will not follow the Lord. That's why he tempts us in so many things. You need to do the right thing and tell your parents the truth. Read 1 Corinthians 10:13 again. Also, remember that the chances are high that your parents will find out the truth anyway, and then you will be in double trouble for lying.

### Questions to ponder:

Tell me about your biggest temptation to do evil.
How did you handle it?

God, lead us not into temptation.

**JOURNAL:**_____

_____

_____

_____

_____

_____

_____

_____

_____

_____

_____

_____

_____

_____

_____

_____

_____

_____

_____

_____

_____

_____

# JANUARY 30

**Q:** I absolutely hate going to the dentist. I would rather go anywhere or do anything else than see the dentist. Any time I need to go, I start shaking, and my stomach goes in knots. I get that nauseating feeling like I'm going to throw up. I don't know what it is, but there's something about the dentist that gives me anxiety, and nothing seems to help calm me down. My mom has tried everything, including buying me a new baseball bat or getting candy after the appointment, but it doesn't help. When I see the dentist's office, I go nuts. I need to figure out how to get rid of this terrible anxiety.

> **What God Says**: Luke 21:34 *Watch out! Don't let me find you filled with the worries of life.**

**A:** Most people get high anxiety going to the dentist or doctor. There's something about the dentist, either the smell or the noise of the drill, that causes us fear. But, in the passage above, God says to cast all anxieties and fears in this world onto Him, and He will give you peace. God is your only salvation from high anxiety. Talk to Him in prayer before going to the dentist's office, and ask Him for courage and strength. Tell Him your anxieties, and then trust Him to help you. If you do this, your anxieties will definitely be minimized.

## Questions to ponder:

Why does going to a dentist give most people anxiety?

How would you try to calm your anxieties?

Cast all your anxieties on the Lord.

**JOURNAL:**

# JANUARY 31

## TEACHER PROBLEMS

**Q:** I have a seventh-grade teacher who hates me. She is always on my case. When all the kids are being loud and talking, she always seems to single me out, and I'm the one who gets in the most trouble. When she's asking questions to the entire class and no one knows the answer, she always seems to pick on me. If anything goes wrong in the classroom, I usually get blamed for it. For instance, last week there was a bunch of kids throwing wads of paper across the room, and instead of all of us getting in trouble, I got blamed for starting it, even though I didn't. Then, when I don't do well on a test, it seems like she enjoys giving me a bad grade. I truly don't know what to do.

> **What God Says**: Romans 13:4 *The authorities are sent by God to help you. But if you are doing wrong, of course you should be afraid for you will be punished. The authorities are established by God for that purpose to punish those who do wrong.*\*

**A:** Authorities are put in place for a reason, and that is to keep the laws sacred and to discipline those who don't obey the laws. They are there to help us in any way they can and make sure things are done right. However, if authority figures overstep their bounds, they will be subject to God's judgment. You need to read Romans 13:4 again so you can totally understand your teacher's role. Then, go talk to her in private—humbly, respectfully—and explain your frustrations. God has a way of making every impossible situation positive.

### Questions to ponder:
Has there ever been a teacher that you didn't like?

Why?

How did you handle that teacher?

Respect your authorities.

**JOURNAL:**

**The life lessons I have learned this month are:**

_____

_____

_____

_____

_____

_____

_____

_____

_____

_____

_____

_____

_____

_____

_____

_____

_____

_____

_____

_____

_____

_____

_____

# FEBRUARY 1

## HELPING KIDS WHO MAKE A BIG MISTAKE

**Q:** I have a good friend who goes to church every Sunday and is a good Christian kid. But last week while he was at the mall, he did something really dumb. Without thinking, he went into a sporting goods store and stole a pair of expensive Nike tennis shoes. As he was walking out, a security guard stopped him and busted him for stealing the shoes. I don't understand why he did it. He has plenty of shoes, and he has never done anything like that before. He is not only in trouble with the law, but also with his parents. Also, his good name and reputation were destroyed. He is facing all these consequences over a lousy pair of tennis shoes. He's in total despair, and I would like to help him out, but I don't know what to do.

**What God Says:** Exodus 2:12 *After looking around to make sure that no one was watching, Moses killed the Egyptian and buried him in the sand.\**

**A:** Unfortunately, we all are sinners, and we all make mistakes. Some mistakes are larger than others, but God does not condemn us when we make mistakes. Look at the life of Moses. Even he, the great servant of our Lord, was marred by an immature, terrible mistake. That mistake is mentioned in Exodus 2:12 quoted above. The key for your friend is to first ask God for forgiveness, make amends by paying for the shoes or returning them to the store, and apologize. Then, your friend should promise not to ever make the same mistake again. Remember, we all make mistakes and God forgives us, but we must not make the same mistakes again.

### Question to ponder:

How do you help friends who make a big mistake?

Turn to God for forgiveness.

**JOURNAL:**

_____

_____
_____
_____
_____
_____
_____
_____
_____
_____
_____
_____
_____
_____
_____
_____
_____
_____
_____
_____
_____
_____
_____

# FEBRUARY 2

## HANDLING A CRISIS

**Q:** I'm only in the eighth grade, but I seem to have a lot of homework. It's already Saturday night, and by Monday morning, I have two term papers due and have to study for a big test. I've been working on the term papers, but I keep starting over because they don't sound very good. I'm in a big panic, and this crisis is going to kill me. I shouldn't have waited until the last minute to begin. It's just that time flies by, and all my classes are giving more and more homework. I really need some help getting over this major crisis.

> **What God Says:** Proverbs 27:12 *A prudent person foresees the danger ahead and takes precautions. The simpleton goes blindly on and suffers the consequence.**

**A:** I think what God is saying to you in this verse is that you should have been a little more organized in starting your assignments and probably should have started them earlier. The first thing God suggests is to relax. Then, get yourself organized, say a prayer asking Him for calmness to clear your head, and start working. The worst thing you can do is panic, because it gains you nothing, and it costs you a ton of wasted energy. As long as you do things in an organized fashion, they will be much easier for you to manage.

### Questions to ponder:
How do you handle a crisis in your life?
Do you ask God for help?

Keep up with your responsibilities
before they become a crisis.

**JOURNAL:**

# FEBRUARY 3

## HELPING KIDS DEAL WITH REJECTION

**Q:** Sometimes, my friends and I try to act real cool and start picking on the smaller, quieter kids at school. I know it's not right, but we truly don't mean any harm. We do it all for fun. However, one day, my friend suddenly decided he didn't want to do that anymore. I don't know what changed him, but he wouldn't participate in our jokes and insults. Once this happened, the other kids in the group started to ignore him to the point of totally rejecting him from being with us. Now, my friend sits alone at lunch, dejected and feeling rejected. I'd like to help him out, but I don't want to be rejected, too.

**What God Says:** 2 Corinthians 12:10 *Since I know it is all for Christ's good, I am quite content with my weakness and with insults, hardships, persecutions, and calamities. For when I am weak, then I am strong.*\*

**A:** I'm not exactly sure how to explain your friend's change of behavior, but I guarantee you that he is walking with the Lord more than the rest of you guys. Have your friend read the above verse over and over again. It's the perfect solution for his situation. He may feel rejected by everyone at this moment, but the great thing is knowing that his loving father in heaven accepts him with open arms. No one, including you, needs mean friends. You are telling me that you want to help your friend. You tell me that you have a compassionate heart. So, it would seem that both of you guys would be better off finding new friends. Give your friend as much comfort and support as you can, and take the risk of hanging out with new friends.

**Question to ponder:**

How do you handle a friend with a broken heart?

God will heal a rejected/dejected heart.

**JOURNAL:** _____

_____

_____

_____

_____

_____

_____

_____

_____

_____

_____

_____

_____

_____

_____

_____

_____

_____

_____

_____

_____

_____

_____

_____

# FEBRUARY 4

## REVENGE

**Q:** I have a good friend who is small and shy, but he's a really nice kid. The other day, a group that is known for being bullies in the neighborhood came up to my friend and pushed him down and then punched him in the face. They broke his glasses and took off with his scooter. He was upset because the scooter was his only means of transportation since his bike was broken. He was cut up pretty bad, and his face was badly bruised. After I saw him, I was really angry. I wanted to get revenge on those bullies in the worst way. I wanted to go beat them up and steal their bikes to make them pay for what they did to my friend. I know that revenge is not the right thing to do, but these kids need to be taught a lesson, or they'll just do it again.

> **What God Says:** Romans 12:19 *Dear friends, never avenge yourselves. Leave that to God. For it is written, "I will take vengeance, and I will repay those who deserve it, says the Lord."*

**A:** The best advice to give here is to leave the revenge in God's hands, for He is the judge of our universe. I know how you feel. You're angry with what those mean kids did to your friend. You saw the fear and anger in your friend's eyes, and you want revenge. You want those kids to feel the same pain. Read the above verse again. God promises to get revenge on evil people. I agree that a crime like this against your friend must be brought to justice, but personal revenge starts an endless cycle of sin and destruction. Let God take care of those bullies.

## Questions to ponder:

Would you seek revenge if your friend was beat up by bullies?
Why or why not?

God will take care of the wicked in His way.

**JOURNAL:**

# WITNESSING

**Q:** I really want to tell my friends about Jesus, but I'm afraid. I was not a Christian until last year when a friend of mine invited me to church one Sunday morning. I really enjoyed the service and went back the following week. Now, I go every Sunday, and I started getting involved in Tuesday night youth group. Just last month, I made my decision to turn my life completely over to Christ and was baptized. I'm really excited about that, and I want to tell all my friends, but I'm afraid I'll say something wrong or that I won't be able to answer any of their questions. I'm still kind of new at this and don't know everything I should know. I am mostly worried that instead of helping my friends grow closer to God, I will actually turn them further away from Him. I know my heart is in the right place, but my head is extremely confused.

> **What God Says:** Luke 21:15 *I will give you the right words and such wisdom that none of your opponents will be able to reply.*\*

**A:** The first thing you need to do is pray to God and trust Him to give you the right words to say, as He promises in the verse above. When you get baptized, you are filled with the Holy Spirit who helps you get over that fear of witnessing. The best way to tell people about Jesus is through your own personal testimony. Show them how you came to know Christ and the difference it has made in your life. There is nothing more powerful than a personal testimony that comes from the heart. If your friends have questions you can't answer, refer them to a pastor at your church, or try to find the answers yourself.

## Questions to ponder:

Why is it so difficult for kids to witness about God?

Why is God such a forbidden subject?

God calls all of us to be witnesses to His word.

**JOURNAL:** _____

_____
_____
_____
_____
_____
_____
_____
_____
_____
_____
_____
_____
_____
_____
_____
_____
_____
_____
_____
_____
_____
_____
_____
_____
_____
_____

# FEBRUARY 6

## HELPING KIDS WHO CAN'T FOCUS

**Q:** There is a kid in my class who just can't seem to focus on any subject. He is not dumb by any means. He just can't sit still while the teacher is talking. He disrupts the class on a daily basis, and he doesn't pay attention to the teacher. His parents had him tested for ADD about a year ago, but it turned out negative. Unfortunately, his parents and teachers have come up with no solutions except possibly putting him in a special school for handicapped kids. I'm not sure whether this kid is a troublemaker who is not interested in school or just not able to focus, but I do know he needs help.

> **What God Says:** Hebrews 12:13 *Mark out a straight path for your feet. Then those who follow you, though they are weak and lame, will not stumble and fall but will become strong.*

**A:** If this child does not have ADD and can't focus, then he does need some medical attention for a learning disorder. Being able to focus in school or in life is critical in order to be successful with God. In the verse above, God teaches us to make goals for ourselves and focus on the right path. If we do this, we will not stumble and fall, but it all starts with God. Ask your friend to pray to God to clear his mind and focus on what is being said. He shouldn't think about anything else and allow his mind to focus on the instruction. God will help him if he allows God into his heart.

### Questions to ponder:
How do you help friends who struggle with focus?

Focus on God, for He will lead you
down the right path.

**JOURNAL:** _____

_____

_____

_____

_____

_____

_____

_____

_____

_____

_____

_____

_____

_____

_____

_____

_____

_____

_____

_____

_____

# FEBRUARY 7

## ACCOUNTABILITY

**Q:** I am in a seventh-grade science project with three other kids. We were each supposed to do one part of the science project. One person was to get all the materials necessary to do the experiment, one person was assigned to do the experiment accurately, another person was supposed to gather the data on a daily basis, and the last person was to write the actual paper. My job was to record the data at home, and I didn't. I would come home from school and get involved in other things and forget to gather the data for that day. We tried to make up some data, but the teacher knew it wasn't accurate, so he gave the entire team a D for the project. It was all my fault. I should have gotten the D, not the other kids.

> **What God Says:** Romans 14:12 *Yes, each of us will have to give a personal account to God.*\*

**A:** It was definitely your fault that the group got a D on the science project. You were lazy and irresponsible, and it gave your friends and yourself a bad grade. God will hold us all accountable for everything we do here on earth. To make up for your mistake, you must make amends by telling the teacher exactly what happened, and hopefully, your friends will get a second chance at a better grade, or the teacher will reconsider grading the entire group the same. Do the right thing, and do whatever is possible to make up for this unfortunate incident.

## Questions to ponder:

How are you accountable to God?

What does God expect from you?

We are all accountable to God for our deeds.

**JOURNAL:** _____

_____
_____
_____
_____
_____
_____
_____
_____
_____
_____
_____
_____
_____
_____
_____
_____
_____
_____
_____
_____
_____
_____
_____

# FEBRUARY 8

## FAITHLESSNESS

**Q:** I play baseball for our eighth-grade class, and one day, I left the baseball field and forgot my glove in the dugout. I went back to try to find it, but it was gone. I had my name on it, so I figured that whoever found it would return it to me, but no one returned it. It was an authentic Ken Griffey Jr. outfielder glove with a deep pocket. It was the best mitt I've ever seen. My parents keep telling me to have faith in God that it will be returned, but so far, NOTHING. There is no way I could ever get another mitt like that because it was a collector's glove and would cost over $200, and my parents can't afford to spend that kind of money. I have lost faith in God to help me. Why would He take away something that I love so much?

> **What God Says:** Hebrews 11:1 *What is faith? It is the confident assurance that what we hope for is going to happen.*\*

**A:** You should never lose faith in God, because that faith is the only hope you've got. Once we lose faith in God, we lose all hope in life. Just because your glove hasn't turned up yet does not mean you have to lose faith. Always remember that God loves us and will never leave us. He also works in mysterious ways for those who believe in Him. When one door closes (losing the glove), we feel dismayed and hopeless, but God opens up another door that could be better than before. Read the verse above and keep praying and putting your faith in your father in heaven.

## Questions to ponder:
How strong is your faith?

In what areas could it be stronger?

Without faith in God, we have nothing.

**JOURNAL:** _____

_____
_____
_____
_____
_____
_____
_____
_____
_____
_____
_____
_____
_____
_____
_____
_____
_____
_____
_____
_____
_____
_____
_____
_____

# FEBRUARY 9

## COMPARING ONE KID TO ANOTHER

**Q:** I have an older brother whom I love very much. We have a lot of fun together fishing and playing sports, and he's a great guy. He is also very good at everything. He gets straight As in all his classes, and he's captain of his football team. He was also the eighth-grade class president. I'm two years younger, and I'm not so good at anything. I barely get passing grades, and I'm not very athletic or popular. The problem is that my parents are always comparing me to my brother and judging my abilities against his. They always say how great he is and how average or worse I am. It is really starting to bug me. Why do parents compare one kid to another? Aren't we all unique in our own way?

> **What God Says:** Proverbs 24:23 *"It is wrong to show favoritism when passing judgment."*

**A:** You are absolutely right that it is totally wrong to compare, judge, or show favoritism for one child over another. God made all people equal, and God loves all of His people equally. In God's eyes, no person is better than another. In the verse above, God states bluntly how wrong it is to show favoritism. You need to tell your parents how you feel, and hopefully, they will see that they are wrong and correct it. Then, figure out what you do well and work hard to be the best at it, no matter what that is. In this way, you can identify the talents that God has bestowed on you.

### Question to ponder:

Why, in your opinion, is showing favoritism for one child over another wrong?

Never judge others unfairly
lest you be judged.

**JOURNAL:**

_____

_____

_____

_____

_____

_____

_____

_____

_____

_____

_____

_____

_____

_____

_____

_____

_____

_____

_____

_____

_____

# TRUTH ABOUT THE BIBLE

**Q:** I just started the ninth grade at a new public school. I've been raised as a Christian, and I believe in the Bible and Jesus Christ as the truth. This school is full of kids with different beliefs. There are Muslims, Jehovah's Witnesses, and Buddhists, and they are all telling me that the Bible is a fairy tale and that the book they believe in is the one true book. They have convincing arguments for their beliefs, and now I'm getting confused. I'm not sure if this is a temptation from the devil to turn me away from the Bible and toward false prophets, or maybe they have a point and the Bible is just a bunch of interesting stories. How do I know for sure that the Bible is the true way to heaven?

> **What God Says:** Psalm 119:160 *All your words are true;*
> *all your just laws will stand forever.*\*

**A:** The easiest way to answer your question is that God says so. The Bible is an extension of God's true character. No other book has withstood the test of time. I do think that the devil is using these kids at school to get you to question your faith in the Bible. This is a test of faith, and you need to pray to God to withstand this test and keep your faith in the Bible strong. Always remember that God wrote the Bible through people so we might believe in Him. As Psalm 119:160 says, all the words in the Bible are true, and God's laws will stand forever.

## Questions to ponder:

Do you really believe that the Bible is true?
Why or why not?

The Bible is the source of God's word.

**JOURNAL:** _____

_____

_____

_____

_____

_____

_____

_____

_____

_____

_____

_____

_____

_____

_____

_____

_____

_____

_____

_____

_____

# HELPING FRIENDS WHO QUESTION PARENTS' LOVE

**Q:** My best friend at school has some serious family problems. Both of her parents work 60 hours a week, six days a week. They really don't need the money because they live in a nice house with two nice cars and money in the bank. When they finally do get home, they are always tired and never want to spend any time with her. My friend makes all the meals, does all the laundry, takes care of her brothers and sisters, and basically takes care of the house. There are times when her parents leave town for a few days, leaving my 12-year-old friend responsible for the family. Her parents never show gratitude to her, and they never tell her they love her. My friend loves her parents, but she questions whether they love her.

> **What God Says:** 1 Timothy 5:8 *But those who won't care for their own relatives, especially those living in the same household, have denied what we believe. Such people are worse than unbelievers.*\*

**A:** I can't believe how your friend's parents isolate themselves from their kids. It makes you wonder why they had children in the first place if they love their jobs so much. Parents have a responsibility to care for and love their children, and that should be their primary priority. That is what God expects of them. Your friend needs to voice her feelings to her parents and let them know how she feels. God uses very strong language in the passage above regarding people (especially parents) who don't seem to love or care about their kids. Make sure she gets this situation resolved quickly, because it will do tremendous damage to your friend in the long run.

### Questions to ponder:

When do you question your parents' love for you?

How do you get over that thought?

Parents are expected to care for
and love their children.

**JOURNAL:**

_____

_____

_____

_____

_____

_____

_____

_____

_____

_____

_____

_____

_____

_____

_____

_____

_____

_____

_____

_____

_____

## CHOICES

**Q:** Don't you hate it when you have two things happening on the same night? That's the dilemma facing me, and I don't know what to do. I've been practicing with the kids' choir the past month for a church performance next week. Then, I found out that on the same day at the same time, I was invited to a real cool party that I would just die to go to. I really want to go to the party, but I also don't want to let my choir friends down at church. I know that the right thing to do is to go to the choir performance, but if I miss the party, I'll be considered the biggest geek in school. I really don't know what to do.

> **What God Says:** Matthew 16:26 *How do you benefit if you gain the whole world but lose your own soul in the process? Is anything worth more than your soul?**

**A:** At your young age, you do have a difficult choice to make. Read Matthew 16:26 again. What it means is that if we let our choices be guided by a desire to gain the world, then we are probably going to make the wrong choices. I agree that going to the party will probably gain you popularity, attention, and a lot of (worldly) fun, but participating in the church choir will gain you popularity and attention from God. The best scenario would be to go to both, but if they are at the same time, that obviously won't work. I would probably choose the church choir because there will always be other parties, and I would rather serve the Lord than serve the world.

## Questions to ponder:

Why do most kids choose what is wrong over what is right?
Do you consult God before making a decision?

Make the right choice. Live for God.

**JOURNAL:** _____

_____

_____

_____

_____

_____

_____

_____

_____

_____

_____

_____

_____

_____

_____

_____

_____

_____

_____

_____

_____

_____

_____

# FEBRUARY 13

## LACK OF TALENT

**Q:** It seems to me that all my friends have a lot more talent than I do. They either get good grades in school, do really well in sports, or play an instrument beautifully. I can't do any of these things, and it's frustrating watching them excel at their talents when I don't excel at anything. I truly don't think I have any talents, and it's not like I haven't tried. I went out for many sports activities, and I have hobbies such as skating and skateboarding. The problem is that I'm not very coordinated, so I just can't do any of those things well. My parents urge me to try different things, but I think it's hopeless. Why did God give everyone but me a ton of talent?

> **What God Says:** Romans 12:6 *God has given each of us the ability to do certain things well.*\*

**A:** God made us all different. God has given some people obvious talents in sports and music. But for others, God has given talents that are not quite so obvious. For example, serving, compassion, or having a good speaking voice are also talents and gifts from God. But rest assured that God has given each and every one of us talents to use in this world to glorify Him. We just need to find out what they are. The best way to accomplish that is to write down all your good qualities and look for a pattern of things you do well. Chances are you will find your hidden talents sooner than you think. Trust God, and He will lead you.

## Questions to ponder:
What are your top three talents?
How are you using those talents to glorify God?

Use your talents to glorify God.

**JOURNAL:**

_____

_____

_____

_____

_____

_____

_____

_____

_____

_____

_____

_____

_____

_____

_____

_____

_____

_____

_____

_____

_____

_____

_____

# HELPING FRIENDS WHO GRUMBLE

**Q:** I have a good friend who always seems to be grumbling negative things about her mom. She's a good kid, and she has a great mom. Every time we go to her house, her mom has cookies for us to snack on. But when her mom says no to my friend, especially when they are at the mall or a department store, all my friend does is grumble mean things about her mom. It really frustrates me because I like her mom a lot, and I don't like to hear those terrible things. Sometimes, I think my friend is a little spoiled, so when she doesn't get her way, she gets mad and grumbles about it. What can I do to get my friend to stop grumbling about her mom without risking my friendship with her?

**What God Says:** Phillipians 2:14 *"Do everything without complaining and arguing."*

**A:** Grumbling mean things about anyone is a total waste of time. God abhors those who grumble for no good reason. And trust me, God has heard a ton of grumbling over the years. From the Israelites in the desert (Exodus) to the Pharisees and religious scholars in Jesus's time (the Gospels), people seem to love to grumble. Tell your friend to be thankful for everything she has and to be thankful for God's blessings. Tell her to stop being so spoiled and to be grateful for her mother. As a friend, you have the responsibility to be honest, as long as it is done in a loving and positive way. She may not realize this fault and would be grateful that you pointed it out to her.

**Questions to ponder:**
What is wrong with grumbling when you are mad?
Why is it a sin?

> Grumbling is a useless sin.

**JOURNAL:**

_____

_____

_____

_____

_____

_____

_____

_____

_____

_____

_____

_____

_____

_____

_____

_____

_____

_____

_____

_____

_____

_____

_____

# FEBRUARY 15

## DEALING WITH UNPOPULAR KIDS

**Q:** There is a kid on my street who seems to always be picked on by all the other neighborhood boys. He is pretty quiet and shy, and sometimes he dresses like a nerd. He has to wear prescription glasses that are pretty thick, and he doesn't wear the coolest clothes. The neighborhood boys tease him a lot, and when we are playing a game on the street, he never gets picked by either team. But he's a really nice kid, and sometimes I feel really bad for him. He tells me it doesn't bother him, but I can tell it really does bother him. I'd like to help him out, but I'm not big enough to fight his battles, nor do I want to be called names just for trying to help him. What should I do?

> **What God Says:** Matthew 5:44 *"Love your enemies! Pray for those who persecute you!"*

**A:** Matthew 5:44 is extremely difficult to understand. How is it possible to love someone when they are laughing at you, making fun of you, or hitting you? God doesn't say to love what they do but to love the person as a child of God. Your friend needs to forgive those who treat him badly and pray for them to change their ways. I know it's easier said than done, especially when you are the one getting persecuted, but if he does that, his reward in heaven will be great. As a Christian kid, you need to be a friend to this young man and not be mean like the others. It is much easier to love your enemies when you have the support of a true friend.

## Questions to ponder:

How do you handle nerds at your school or in your neighborhood? Do you treat them differently?

Let God take care of your enemies.

**JOURNAL:** _____

_____
_____
_____
_____
_____
_____
_____
_____
_____
_____
_____
_____
_____
_____
_____
_____
_____
_____
_____
_____
_____
_____
_____

# CRITICIZING

**Q:** I have a major problem with my mouth. It seems like I'm always criticizing authority. It doesn't matter if it's my teachers, my parents, my soccer coach, or even my older brother, I am always very critical of the things they do. I think the problem is that I am very critical of people who think differently than I do. When I think someone has done something wrong, I go around and tell others what I think. When it gets back to them that I was criticizing their words or behavior, I usually get in big trouble. It's really strange, but I can't get over this habit. I know that I'm not perfect, and I don't like it when people criticize me, but I still do it anyway. I know I need to stop, but I just don't know how.

**What God Says:** Romans 14:10 *Why do you condemn (criticize) another Christian? Remember, each of us will stand before the judgment seat of God.**

**A:** First, it is important for a child to always respect those in authority and not be openly critical of them. Sometimes, kids have a hard time under-standing why parents, teachers, or coaches do or say certain things. But most of the time, if what the adults say or do is different from the way kids think, it is for the kids' good. As a child, you have no right to be critical of anybody, let alone those people in authority. How do you know that you're right and they're wrong? Who gave you the right to criticize and judge others? God wants us to listen to our elders and not judge them based on their decisions. As the verse says, don't judge or criticize others, or you will be treated the same way.

## Questions to ponder:

What do you think about kids who are critical of others?

How do you deal with them?

Unnecessary criticism leads to hardships.

**JOURNAL:**_____

_____

_____

_____

_____

_____

_____

_____

_____

_____

_____

_____

_____

_____

_____

_____

_____

_____

_____

_____

_____

_____

_____

_____

# FEBRUARY 17

## DEALING WITH FRIENDS WHO HAVE FEAR

**Q:** My good friend lives in a rough part of town. There is a lot of crime and gangs in her neighborhood, and it scares her to death. She lives with her mom and two sisters. Her mom is currently working two jobs just so they can live where they are now. So unfortunately, they cannot afford to move out of the neighborhood. My friend can't go outside after dark, and she sometimes has a difficult time sleeping because of the gunshots and sirens. Every night, she lives in fear that someone is going to rob them or that they may become innocent victims of a drive-by shooting. With all the drugs and gangs that hang out around her apartment complex, it's a definite possibility.

**What God Says:** Isaiah 41:10 *Don't be afraid for I am with you. Do not be dismayed for I am your God. I will strengthen you. I will help you. I will uphold you with my victorious right hand.\**

**A:** Your friend is in a difficult situation, and it would be wonderful if she could move out of that rough neighborhood. But for now, your friend needs to accept the things she cannot change and try to make the best of it. You need to remind your friend that her family is not alone in that apartment and that God is watching over them. They need to understand that God is stronger than any rough neighborhood, and He wants to use His strength to help us. You need to tell your friend to pray to God to give her courage, strength, and peace of mind. Make sure they are as safety-conscious as possible and that they put their trust in God.

**Question to ponder:**

How do you handle fear in your life?

Give an example of when you were very scared and what you did.

Lean on God when dealing with fear.

**JOURNAL:**
_____

_____
_____
_____
_____
_____
_____
_____
_____
_____
_____
_____
_____
_____
_____
_____
_____
_____
_____
_____
_____
_____
_____
_____

# FEBRUARY 18

## STRICT PARENTS

**Q:** I have a really strict dad. He won't allow me to do anything. I'm in the seventh grade, and my friends are allowed to stay up late, watch TV late on weekends, talk on the phone, and even go to the mall with friends. I'm not allowed to do any of those things. I can only talk on the phone for 10 minutes at a time and no later than 8:00 p.m. I must be in bed on school nights no later than 9:00 p.m., and by 9:30 p.m. on weekends. My friends laugh at me and call me "baby" because of my strict dad. Why can't my dad be like all the other dads and not be so strict with me? I do love him, but I think his rigid parenting is way too much.

> **What God Says:** Ephesians 6:4 *And now a word to you fathers. Don't make your children angry by the way you treat them. Rather bring them up with the discipline and instruction approved by the Lord.*\*

**A:** God agrees with discipline as long as it is applied in a godly manner to honor Him and not to make children fear their parents. It sounds like your dad is afraid of something and is being overly protective. Talk to your dad in a calm, respectful way and ask him little by little to be more lenient with you. If you show responsibility (good grades, doing chores on time, and more), rest assured that he will be less strict with you. Read Ephesians 6:4 to him. Tell him that you love him but that he needs to be more trusting of you and less rigid.

## Questions to ponder:

What is your opinion of strict parents?

Is there a godly way to discipline?

Always use discipline in a godly manner.

**JOURNAL:** _____

_____

_____

_____

_____

_____

_____

_____

_____

_____

_____

_____

_____

_____

_____

_____

_____

_____

_____

_____

_____

_____

_____

## TRIALS

**Q:** I went to an all-boys camp for the club I belong to. It was up in the mountains where we went hiking and fishing and did other fun activities. It was not a Christian camp, even though I am a Christian kid. The problem was the other boys at camp. They were mostly non-Christians, and all they did was curse, swear, say God's name in vain, vandalize, and say negative things about God. They all wanted me to join them in order to fit in. I felt that my faith was on trial. I acted like I was one of them but tried to stay out of it as much as possible. It was extremely uncomfortable.

**What God Says:** James 1:12 *"God blesses the people who patiently endure testing and temptation. Afterward they will receive the crown of life that God has promised to those who love him."*

**A:** Every person in the world will encounter trials and temptations. The key is how we react when the trials are upon us. God highly blesses those who are laughed at or made fun of because of their faith. My suggestion is to stop hanging out with those kids and try to find a club whose members are more Christ-like. I think it would be more comfortable for you in the long run, and you can have just as much fun without being tempted to be evil.

### Questions to ponder:

How do you usually react when faced with a difficult trial?

Do you turn to God for help?

Make sure you are innocent in your trials
with God.

**JOURNAL:**_____

_____

_____

_____

_____

_____

_____

_____

_____

_____

_____

_____

_____

_____

_____

_____

_____

_____

_____

_____

_____

_____

_____

_____

# FEBRUARY 20

## DEALING WITH FORGETFUL PEOPLE

**Q:** I have a problem with my mom. She is a wonderful person and a loving mother, but she has a terrible memory. Believe it or not, every year she forgets my birthday unless I remind her the week before. If I ask her for help on something ahead of time or ask her to buy me something for a class project the next week, she forgets. I've tried everything, including writing notes to remind her, but she still forgets. One time, she forgot to pick my friend and me up at the mall, and we had to wait over two hours for her to get there. She's a single mom and she does work a lot, but I think that's more of an excuse. I don't know what more I can do to jog her memory on things involving me.

> **What God Says:** Isaiah 49:15 *Can a mother forget her nursing child? Can she feel no love for a child she has borne? But even if that was possible, I would never forget you.*

**A:** There should be nothing more important for a mom than her child. I have a hard time understanding what could be more important to a mom than picking up her kid at a mall or celebrating her child's birthday. God says in the above verse that it is despicable for a mother not to remember her child. And you're right! Having to work or being a single mom is no excuse. I suggest that you continue with your reminders on a consistent basis until your mom learns to remember things on her own. Get your mom a journal or a daily planner in which you can write important dates. And sit down and tell her how you feel and how sad it makes you when she forgets you.

### Questions to ponder:

How do you deal with forgetful people?
How do you try to help them?

Don't forget about God's children,
or God may forget about you.

**JOURNAL:** _____

_____

_____

_____

_____

_____

_____

_____

_____

_____

_____

_____

_____

_____

_____

_____

_____

_____

_____

_____

_____

# FEBRUARY 21

## BAD HABITS

**Q:** I have this terrible habit of butting into another person's business. I feel like I have a solution to every problem, but I really don't. I don't do this to be a show-off or a know-it-all. I truly want to help people with their problems. So, whenever I see a group of kids or just two kids talking, I always get involved in the conversation by inserting my opinion even though no one asked for it. Then, the kids usually get mad at me, and I feel bad. I know it becomes very annoying for my friends at school, but I don't know how to stop myself. What can I do to teach myself to mind my own business?

> **What God Says:** Proverbs 26:17 *Yanking a dog's ears is as foolish as interfering in someone else's argument.*\*

**A:** This verse is God's way of saying in a nice way to mind your own business. Normally, someone full of pride feels they always have solutions to other people's problems. Or sometimes, a person needs to be the center of attention no matter what the situation is or no matter who's speaking. How would you like it if someone constantly butted in on your private conversations to give you their opinion? God teaches us that it is wrong to do this, and you need to exercise self-control and not involve yourself in another person's business. Pray to God to give you the strength and will-power to do that.

**Questions to ponder:**
What are some of your bad habits?
How do you try to fix them?

Bad habits are hard to break.
Ask God for help.

**JOURNAL:** _____

_____

_____

_____

_____

_____

_____

_____

_____

_____

_____

_____

_____

_____

_____

_____

_____

_____

_____

_____

_____

_____

# FEBRUARY 22

## MATERIALISM

**Q:** I really love my skateboard and inline skates. I love them more than anything else in the world. When I'm not in school or doing homework, I'm either skating or boarding. I would do it 24 hours a day, seven days a week if I could. I skate around my neighborhood or go to the park and skate with my friends. I don't know what I would do if my skateboard or skates were lost or stolen. I worry about these two objects more than I worry about myself. There is nothing I won't do to make sure that these two things are safe. I usually sleep with my skates and my skateboard on my bed.

> **What God Says:** Acts 14:15 *"We have come to bring you the Good News that you should turn from these worthless things to the living God, who made heaven and earth, the sea, and everything in them."*

**A:** Your love for materialistic objects is truly quite scary. It is what the Bible calls idolizing false gods. You are treating your skateboard and your skates like idols, and that is extremely dangerous. There is only one thing you should love that much, and that's God. Keep in mind that God is the one who created the skateboard and the skates and provided them to you to enjoy here on earth. They technically belong to Him. Turn your adoration for these material items over to the Lord, who gives you everything.

**Questions to ponder:**
What are three of your favorite things to own?
Do you treat them better than your Bible?

You can't take your things to heaven.

**JOURNAL:** _____

_____

_____

_____

_____

_____

_____

_____

_____

_____

_____

_____

_____

_____

_____

_____

_____

_____

_____

_____

_____

_____

# FEBRUARY 23

## SALVATION QUESTIONS

**Q:** I am a Christian, and I do believe in Jesus Christ as my Lord and savior. But most of my friends are non-Christians. I have Jewish friends who do not believe in Jesus. I have Mormon friends who believe in a man named Joseph Smith as their spiritual leader. I even have atheist friends who don't believe in any god. All of them (except the atheists) believe they are going to heaven, but none of them believe in Jesus. They are all good kids who are nice to everyone, and I want them to experience salvation in heaven. How do I know they won't be saved? How do I know that my religion is the only faith that will get you to heaven?

> **What God Says:** Romans 10:9 *If you confess with your mouth that Jesus is Lord and believe in your heart that God raised Him from the dead, you will be saved.*\*

**A:** The way we know for sure is that God tells us so. Read Romans 10:9 again. God tells us that we must believe in our hearts that Christ is Lord, that He died for our sins, and that is the way to heaven and salvation. Other religions do not teach that faith in Christ as our savior is the only way to heaven. There are many other references in the Bible that teach us the same thing (John 14:6, Matt. 17:5). You need to point your friends to Jesus so they can experience eternal salvation in heaven with God.

### Questions to ponder:
What do you think is the way to heaven?
What are you doing about it?

No one can come to the father
except through Jesus.

**JOURNAL:**

_____
_____
_____
_____
_____
_____
_____
_____
_____
_____
_____
_____
_____
_____
_____
_____
_____
_____
_____
_____
_____

# FEBRUARY 24

## DEALING WITH COCKY KIDS

**Q:** There is a kid in my class who is extremely cocky. All he does all the time is brag about everything he has, how big of a mansion he lives in, and how his mom and dad both drive expensive cars. He brags about all the things he has in his bedroom (TV, DVD, Play Station II) and that his family has horses. When we go back to school after summer vacation or the Christmas holiday, he brags about where he has been on vacation, such as skiing in the Alps during the winter or trips to Europe during the summer. He's just cocky about everything. He drives everyone crazy. What can I do to stop him from being so cocky?

> **What God Says:** Matthew 23:12 *"Those who exalt themselves will be humbled, and those who humble themselves will be exalted."*

**A:** Unfortunately, there isn't a whole lot you can do about someone who is that cocky and arrogant. He probably won't listen to you because he thinks he knows it all. Jesus Christ is the perfect example of humility. He came to this earth in the most humble surroundings, being born in a barn. As God, Jesus could have been as cocky as He wanted, but instead, He came to earth to serve others and not be served. God is very clear that the humble will be saved, but the cocky will not. You either need to ignore this cocky kid or lead by example, showing him how he can gain more friends by being humble like Jesus rather than being full of himself.

## Questions to ponder:

How do you deal with cocky kids?

Why do you think kids get so cocky?

Cockiness will not get you
into the kingdom of God.

**JOURNAL:** _____

_____
_____
_____
_____
_____
_____
_____
_____
_____
_____
_____
_____
_____
_____
_____
_____
_____
_____
_____
_____
_____

# FEBRUARY 25

## DECISION-MAKING

**Q:** I have a good friend at school who has a huge problem. She's only 13 years old, and she's pregnant. She made a mistake trying to act like she was 16 and had sex with an older boy. She made me swear not to tell anyone about this, especially her parents or mine. She's planning on getting an abortion. She really doesn't want an abortion because she knows it's wrong, but she is deathly afraid of what her parents might do to her. Emotionally, she is a wreck. She doesn't eat or sleep, and she's getting sick day after day. She really needs help, but I swore not to tell anyone. I don't know what I should do. Do I betray her trust, break my promise, and tell someone so she can get help? Or do I let her keep suffering and get the abortion?

> **What God Says:** Romans 2:18 *Yes, you know what He wants; you know right from wrong because you have been taught the law.**

**A:** Wow! What a terrible predicament to be in at such a young age. You never want to betray a good friend's trust, but you also don't want her to get hurt or do the wrong thing that will haunt her the rest of her life. The first thing you must do is read God's word for His wisdom. Pray to God to help you with this tough decision. But as God says in the verse above, you know right from wrong. Abortion is wrong, and your friend definitely needs help. Think about this. Sometimes, breaking a promise you made to a friend could save a life or two.

**Questions to ponder:**
What do you do when you have to make a critical decision?
Who do you go to for advice?

Trust God with your difficult decisions.

**JOURNAL:** _____

_____

_____

_____

_____

_____

_____

_____

_____

_____

_____

_____

_____

_____

_____

_____

_____

_____

_____

_____

_____

_____

_____

_____

_____

# PRAYERS NOT ANSWERED

**Q:** I've got a problem with my dad. He's got a terrible drinking problem, but he won't admit that he has this problem. Every night, he either comes home from the bar drunk or he drinks at home until he passes out. Every night when I pray, I ask God to help my dad to stop drinking, but so far, nothing has changed. I have been praying about this for a couple of months but to no avail. I don't think God is listening to my prayers. Why hasn't He helped my dad with this problem? It's not like I'm asking something for myself like a new bike or new skates. This prayer stuff is just not working!

> **What God Says:** Luke 18:1 *One day Jesus told his disciples a story to illustrate their need for constant prayer and to show them that they should never give up.*\*

**A:** First of all, I want you to understand that God listens to all prayers, and He answers every prayer. Just because things are not changing quickly the way we want doesn't mean He's not listening. It's just that we want everything to be done now and fast, and sometimes our timing and God's timing are not the same. But remember, God's timing is always perfect. Don't lose faith! Keep praying to God consistently and persistently about this important issue. In His perfect timing, He will give you the desires of your heart. You just need to trust Him.

## Questions to ponder:

What is something you've been praying for that has not been answered? How often do you pray?

Never give up on God.

**JOURNAL:** _____

_____

_____

_____

_____

_____

_____

_____

_____

_____

_____

_____

_____

_____

_____

_____

_____

_____

_____

_____

_____

_____

_____

_____

_____

## DEALING WITH KIDS WHO DO EVIL

**Q:** A group of us enjoy hanging out together at school. We've known each other since the third grade (five years) and have been very good friends. All of a sudden, one of the kids in the group started acting very strangely. He started acting mean and doing bad things to other kids. He's become very insulting and abusive, and just last week, he tried to get another kid to steal something for him. Lately, he's been lying to everybody, including us, and he's been involved in fights with other boys. Nothing has changed in his life that I know about, so we all don't understand why he is acting so evil. I know inside he's a good kid, but I don't know how to deal with this evil streak.

> **What God Says:** Ezekiel 33:11 *As surely as I live, declares the sovereign LORD, I take no pleasure in the death of the wicked but rather that they turn from their ways and live. Turn! Turn from your evil ways!*\*

**A:** Normally, a major change in a child's behavior is caused by problems in their life. Traumatic situations such as parents divorcing or someone being sick or dying can trigger bitterness inside and make a good kid turn to evil behavior very quickly. But unfortunately, there is no excuse for this type of behavior. Sinning in God's eyes is doing the devil's work. And having other kids do evil for your own gain is terrible. Again, I'm not sure what has caused this transformation, but your friend definitely needs help. Maybe you can talk to his family or someone he admires who can talk some sense into him. The least you need to do is to pray for him. Pray that God will take control of his life and knock the evil spirits out of him.

### Questions to ponder:

Why are there so many evil kids in this world?

How do you deal with them?

God hates all evil.

**JOURNAL:** _____

_____
_____
_____
_____
_____
_____
_____
_____
_____
_____
_____
_____
_____
_____
_____
_____
_____
_____
_____
_____
_____
_____
_____
_____

## DATING

**Q:** I am currently in the eighth grade, and I like this one boy in my class quite a bit. Just last week, to my surprise, he asked me out, and I said yes. I couldn't believe my good fortune. I was so happy until I got home and told my parents. They became angry (dad) and concerned (mom) and basically forbid me to date this boy. They explained that they had heard stories about him from other parents at the school, that he uses girls to get what he wants from them and then brags to his friends about what he accomplished. He's self-centered and a jerk, according to my mom. In my heart, I know he's not that way, but I can't convince my parents to give him a chance and to trust me. This is so not fair!

> **What God Says:** Proverbs 13:10 *Pride leads to arguments; those who take advice are wise.*\*

**A:** In this verse, God is saying that in most cases, your parents know best. They were your age once, and they know about guys with bad reputations. They are just scared that he will hurt you. You probably think you know everything, but that's probably your emotions talking more than your head. If there are stories about this boy, chances are good that they are true. Don't let your pride of being asked out get in the way of good judgment. Do your homework. Check out these stories and see if they are true. If you can prove to your parents that the stories are false, then you'll have a better chance of dating this boy.

## Questions to ponder:

What is a good age to start dating? Why?

What are some problems with dating too young?

Use good judgment before dating.

**JOURNAL:** _____

_____

_____

_____

_____

_____

_____

_____

_____

_____

_____

_____

_____

_____

_____

_____

_____

_____

_____

_____

_____

_____

_____

**The life lessons I have learned this month are:**

_____

_____

_____

_____

_____

_____

_____

_____

_____

_____

_____

_____

_____

_____

_____

_____

_____

_____

_____

_____

_____

_____

_____

_____

# MARCH 1

## LYING

**Q:** I seem to have a terrible problem with lying. I lie to my parents about everything. Sometimes, I lie to my teachers about my homework (the dog ate my worksheet or the rain destroyed my paper), so I don't have to do it. The funny thing is that most of the time, I really don't need to lie. I guess it's the thrill of getting away with something that motivates me to do it. The problem is that it has gotten to the point that I don't know how to tell the truth anymore. I have started lying to my friends at school, and now they don't trust me with anything. What I thought was fun has turned out to be a serious problem. I need to stop lying, but I don't know how.

**What God Says:** Exodus 20:16 *Do not testify falsely against your neighbor.**

**A:** God is extremely clear in the Bible about His stand on lying. He forbids any type of lying to anyone. The verse above is the eighth law of the Ten Commandments. God is all about truth and love, so He hates all lies. You need to change this habit as quickly as possible. You need to get in the habit of telling the truth, even when it gets you into trouble. You need to sit down with someone (probably your parents) who can help you alter this behavior. You need to admit your problem to them and to God and ask for forgiveness. Then, you need to seek forgiveness from everyone else you've lied to. Unless you do that, you will not break this lying behavior.

### Questions to ponder:
Do you have a problem with lying?
What makes you lie?
To whom do you lie the most?

God cannot tolerate a lying tongue.

**JOURNAL:** _____

_____

_____

_____

_____

_____

_____

_____

_____

_____

_____

_____

_____

_____

_____

_____

_____

_____

_____

_____

_____

_____

# MARCH 2

## ACTING BEFORE YOU THINK

**Q:** The other day I was walking home from soccer practice and saw another boy across the street laughing and pointing in my direction. This went on for a few minutes, and it began to irritate me. All of a sudden, without thinking, I crossed the street and punched this kid right in the mouth. It turns out that this kid was laughing and pointing at two dogs who were 50 feet behind me, looking like they were going to have sex. I felt really bad for my actions. I tried to apologize for my stupidity, but it was too late. It was really dumb for me to react like that without thinking. What do I do now?

**What God Says:** Proverbs 13:16 *Wise people think before they act; fools don't and even brag about it.**

**A:** Needless to say, what you did was not very smart. God says it is imperative to always think first, pause, take a deep breath, and make sure anything you say or do is done in the right frame of mind. Planning and foresight will always help us prepare for danger ahead so we can avoid disastrous consequences. Read the verse above again. God teaches us to think before we act, and we are fools if we don't. All you can do now is try to help this kid you hit in any way you can and pray to God that this situation never happens again.

### Questions to ponder:
Why do kids sometimes act before they think?
How can this bad habit be changed?

Always think before you act.

**JOURNAL:** _____

_____

_____

_____

_____

_____

_____

_____

_____

_____

_____

_____

_____

_____

_____

_____

_____

_____

_____

_____

_____

_____

# UNWORTHY OF GOD

**Q:** As I was going through grammar school, I was the all-American kid. I dressed conservatively, and my hair was always short and neat. I was always pleasant and thoughtful, but now that I'm in middle school, things have changed. My clothes have gotten much baggier, my hair is longer and in a ponytail, and my attitude is more confrontational and arrogant. I still feel the same way about God, but since everything about me has changed, seemingly for the worse, I feel I'm not worthy of God's grace. In my two years of middle school, I have sinned more than in six years of elementary school. I'm trying to change back to my old self, but I don't think God will love me the same.

**What God Says:** Colossians 1:21–22 *You were His enemies separated from Him by your evil thoughts and actions, yet now He has brought you back as His friends. He has done this through His death on the cross in His own human body. As a result, He has brought you into the very presence of God, and you are holy and blameless as you stand before Him without a single fault.**

**A:** God will always accept you back, holy and blameless, if you seek Him. That is the beauty of the cross. All your past sins are swept away through the blood of Christ so you can have a fresh start with Him with no guilt or shame. You are God's child whom He loves very much. God will always think you are worthy of His love. All you need to do is accept it in your heart and follow Christ.

**Questions to ponder:**
What does God's grace mean to you?
How has it changed your life?

Thank you, Lord, for sending your son.

**JOURNAL:**

# MARCH 4

## CONFORMING TO WRONG

**Q:** I'm usually a good, thoughtful, positive kid to all people. But sometimes I get caught up with my friends being mean to other kids. It's not peer pressure. There is no one forcing me to be mean to fit in. I do it on my own, because at the time, it seems harmless and fun. For example, the other day, a new kid started at my school, and he looked kind of dorky. Everybody seemed to be laughing at him and insulting him, including me, not by force but by choice. I don't understand why I choose to conform to wrong actions, especially when I know in my heart they are wrong.

> **What God Says:** Romans 12:2 *"Don't copy the behaviors and customs of this world, but let God transform you into a new person by changing the way you think."*

**A:** God expects those who love and follow Him to live by a higher standard with behavior that brings glory to God. We have the perfect model to live by in Christ Jesus. If you are a true believer in God, you must put conscious effort into stopping this evil behavior immediately. Now, I know that we are human. I also know that we make mistakes at times, conforming to what is wrong. However, we need to realize that conforming to evil is Satan's work; we need to ask God for help and guidance to fight off those temptations. God wants us to only conform to good.

### Questions to ponder:
Why do kids conform to wrong?

Have any of your friends started conforming to evil? Explain.

> We need to conform our minds
> and hearts to doing what is good.

**JOURNAL:**

_____

_____

_____

_____

_____

_____

_____

_____

_____

_____

_____

_____

_____

_____

_____

_____

_____

_____

_____

_____

# SIBLING RIVALRY

**Q:** My parents constantly tell me that I need to act more like my brother. My brother is smart, studious, quiet, respectful, and generally well-liked by everybody. I am not as smart as he is, and I am lazy and loud. Sometimes, I get very sassy with my mom. I strive to be a better person, but I will never be like my older brother. I sometimes feel like less of a person or that my parents don't love me as much because I'm not as good as he is. I wish my parents would stop comparing us and making me feel bad.

> **What God Says:** Matthew 18:1–4 *About that time, the disciples came to Jesus and asked, "Which of us is the greatest in the kingdom of heaven?" Jesus said, "Anyone who becomes as humble as this little child is the greatest in the kingdom of heaven."* *

**A:** God looks upon all of us as having equal worth. Competition between siblings is inappropriate anytime because it causes us to rate one child against another. You are no better or no worse than your brother, just different, and God loves both of you exactly the same. You need to ask your parents to stop comparing. Have peace in knowing that God will always love you the same. As Jesus says in the verse above, the humble will be the greatest in God's kingdom.

**Questions to ponder:**

Why do you think sibling rivalry could be dangerous in a home?

Is there sibling rivalry in your home?

God never compares one child to another.

**JOURNAL:**

_____

_____

_____

_____

_____

_____

_____

_____

_____

_____

_____

_____

_____

_____

_____

_____

_____

_____

_____

_____

_____

_____

_____

# MARCH 6

## DISCIPLINE

**Q:** I play middle school basketball, and we recently played our rivals from across town. It's a big deal when the two teams play. My best friend plays forward on our team, and I'm a backup guard. The forward on the other team was playing extremely rough with my friend. He was pushing and shoving most of the game, more than what is usually done in a regular basketball game. Then, in the fourth quarter, he intentionally elbowed my friend right in the face, causing his nose to bleed. Then, he hit him in the eye with his palm. I rushed on the court and hit this guy right in the face with my fist in defense of my friend. Needless to say, I got disciplined with an ejection and a three-game suspension for fighting. I feel this discipline is wrong, because I was only trying to defend my buddy.

> **What God Says:** Proverbs 12:1 *"To learn, you must love discipline; it is stupid to hate correction."*

**A:** I know that all you were trying to do was protect your friend, but the rules of basketball state that anyone who leaves the bench to fight will face disciplinary action. Your intention was for good, but what you did was still wrong. The discipline was necessary because you broke a rule. If you didn't get disciplined, then anyone could come off the bench and hit someone when they feel a teammate is wronged. As the verse above states, we all should learn to love discipline because we can learn from our mistakes. Without discipline, we would make the same mistakes over and over, and we would never learn anything.

## Questions to ponder:

How do you get disciplined at home?

Is it fair?

Why or why not?

Godly discipline is a necessary part of life.

**JOURNAL:** _____

_____
_____
_____
_____
_____
_____
_____
_____
_____
_____
_____
_____
_____
_____
_____
_____
_____
_____
_____
_____
_____
_____
_____
_____

# DEALING WITH KIDS WHO CUSS

**Q:** I have a friend on my baseball team who is always cussing or saying God's name in vain. When the team is doing badly or he is not hitting the ball well, we all get to hear his four-letter words and name-calling, especially to the umpires. The manager of our team and other people have talked to him, but he still cusses constantly. He says it's a bad habit and he means no harm by it, but it is very embarrassing for the team. He's only in the sixth grade. What can I do to get him to stop?

**What God Says:** James 3:2 *We all make many mistakes, but those who control their tongues can also control themselves in every other way.**

**A:** The tongue is a deadly weapon in the eyes of the Lord. It can do as much damage as a sword. The Lord will not tolerate swearing by those who wish to follow Him. You need to talk to your fellow ballplayers, this kid's parents, or any other influential person in his life to help him stop this filthy talk. It doesn't make a person "cool" or "in" or anything good to swear in public. Cussing can lead to other destructive behavior, so he needs guidance as soon as possible.

## Questions to ponder:

How do you deal with kids who cuss?

What do you do when they start cussing?

The tongue can be mightier than the sword.

**JOURNAL:**

# LISTENING TO BAD LYRICS

**Q:** I like Christian music. My friends like to listen to hard rock and rap whenever they are at my house. I listen to soft rock Christian music mostly by Christian bands. The problem is that when I'm with my friends, chilling at their house, they listen to music that is pretty disgusting. Every other word seems like a cuss word, and the lyrics talk about killing, rape, incest, and stealing cars. I already get teased by them for my choice in music, so it's not like I can talk to them about it. I like my friends, but I just don't like their music.

> **What God Says:** Psalm 27:6 *Then I will hold my head high above my enemies who surround me. At His tabernacle, I will offer sacrifices with shouts of joy, singing and praising the LORD with (godly) music.* *

**A:** It seems that if your friends and you differ so greatly in your tastes in music, you probably are also pretty different in your beliefs. God loves music but not music that demeans anyone. Listening to music that talks about murder, rape, incest, or abuse is wrong in God's eyes. Either politely (or as "cool" as possible), ask your buddies not to listen to that stuff when you are around. Or you can find different friends who have more in common with you in their musical tastes. If you don't, your current friends just might influence you away from God.

## Questions to ponder:

What kind of music do you enjoy?

If Jesus were sitting next to you, would He enjoy your music?

Why or why not?

Bad lyrics could lead to bad behavior.

**JOURNAL:** _____

_____
_____
_____
_____
_____
_____
_____
_____
_____
_____
_____
_____
_____
_____
_____
_____
_____
_____
_____
_____
_____
_____
_____

# MARCH 9

## HELPING A FRIEND WHO'S HAVING DOUBTS ABOUT GOD

**Q:** My Christian friend whom I've known for four years (we are 14 now) is starting to have doubts about God. Her cousins are atheists and have been telling her that creation started through evolution and that humans, not God, are the supreme beings on earth. I'm still young in the faith, so I don't know what to say to convince her otherwise. All of a sudden, she stopped going to church or youth group, and any discussion about God now starts an argument between the two of us. Years before, she believed in God and Jesus and went to church faithfully every week, but now everything is in doubt, and I don't know how to convince her otherwise.

> **What God Says:** James 1:6 *But when you ask Him, be sure you really expect Him to answer, for a doubtful mind is as unsettled as a wave in the sea that is driven and tossed by the wind.*\*

**A:** This verse firmly states that if we doubt God, we are tossed around in our faith like waves in the sea and can be easily manipulated and conformed to evil by the devil. We must be strong in our faith and not doubt. You need to hand your friend a Bible and ask her to start reading it again. Literally, thousands of historians and scholars who were atheists and 100% sure that God did not exist have tried to disprove the Bible. But there has not been one person who has been able to find anything untrue in the Bible. Give your friend any book written by a pure atheist that fails to disprove the Bible. That will definitely bring her back to God.

### Questions to ponder:

What questions do your friends have about God?
How do you answer them?

There is no doubt that God exists.

**JOURNAL:**

# MARCH 10

BAPTISM

**Q:** I was excited this past weekend when I made the decision to get baptized. When I went to school to tell my friends this exciting news, most of them said that baptism is a joke and a complete waste of time. They told me that if you love God and do good things, you'll go to heaven. They said baptism was something invented by a religious fanatic, and it really symbolizes nothing. When I tried to argue the point, they just laughed at me and walked away. I feel that baptism is necessary to be a committed Christian, but how do I convince my friends?

> **What God Says:** Mark 16:16 *"Anyone who believes and is baptized will be saved. But anyone who refuses to believe will be condemned."*

**A:** It's very simple. It is in the Bible. God makes it very clear by the verse above as well as many others in the Bible that once you become a follower of Jesus, you need to be baptized in water. Go through your Bible to find other passages on baptism. The Bible even tells us that Jesus was baptized, which proves the major significance of the event. If your friends believe in God, then they must believe in His word.

## Questions to ponder:

What is your opinion on baptism?

Have you been baptized? Why or why not?

144

Baptism solidifies your faith in Christ.

**JOURNAL:** _____

_____
_____
_____
_____
_____
_____
_____
_____
_____
_____
_____
_____
_____
_____
_____
_____
_____
_____
_____
_____
_____

# MARCH 11

## WATCHING TOO MUCH TV

**Q:** When I'm not in school, I'm at home watching TV. I love TV more than anything else in the world. I don't have any hobbies, and I don't enjoy any sports, so I occupy my time watching television. I enjoy watching Disney channel and Nickelodeon and even the Discovery channel. I probably watch TV about four to five hours a day during the school year and nine to 10 hours a day over the summer. My parents are always trying to get me to do other things, but I don't want to. I enjoy television. I'm not hurting anyone, so I don't see the problem. I could watch TV 15 hours a day if I didn't have to go to school.

**What God Says:** 2 Thessalonians 3:6 *We give you this command with the authority of our Lord Jesus Christ. Stay away from any Christian who lives in idleness and doesn't follow the traditions of hard work.\**

**A:** The problem is that God created you in His image and likeness in order to serve Him on this earth. You cannot be serving God or His people if all you do is watch TV all day. God wants you to utilize your talents and the gifts of the Holy Spirit to be productive. You'll never really know what your talents or gifts are unless you look for them. So, stop watching so much TV; find other activities you enjoy, and serve God. As the verse above says, God does not approve of an idle Christian who wastes time being unproductive.

### Questions to ponder:
How many hours of TV do you watch per day?
What do you think God's opinion of TV is today?

Don't be an idle Christian.

**JOURNAL:**

_____

_____

_____

_____

_____

_____

_____

_____

_____

_____

_____

_____

_____

_____

_____

_____

_____

_____

_____

_____

_____

_____

# DISCOURAGED

**Q:** I'm 14 years old. I had not even thought about Christianity until I was eight, when my good friend became a Christian. I was like all the other kids I know. I was loud, disrespectful, always lying, and just obnoxious. So when I gave church a try, I thought it would change my life. From one standpoint, it did. But just the other day, I got caught cheating on a test. Normally, I would lie and get myself out of trouble, but this time, I confessed what I did. Well, I got in big trouble, not only from the teacher but also my parents. I thought doing the right thing would make my life better, but it made it worse. I'm very discouraged and confused that I did the right thing and still got in trouble. So what's the good in being a Christian?

> **What God Says:** Galatians 6:9 *Don't get tired of doing what is good. Don't get discouraged and give up, for we will reap a harvest of blessing at the appropriate time.**

**A:** Remember that being responsible and doing the right thing does not take away from your responsibility for your actions. For every wrongful act, there is a consequence. But when you tell the truth, it shows your courage and good character, and that pleases God. It is human to commit sins, but being honest and feeling sorry for those sins is the mark of a Christian. Be encouraged, not discouraged, by your truthfulness, and keep following God's teachings. Remember, we will receive a great blessing if we follow God's way.

## Questions to ponder:

What discourages you the most?

How do you get over your discouragement?

Don't be discouraged for doing the right thing.

**JOURNAL:** _____

_____
_____
_____
_____
_____
_____
_____
_____
_____
_____
_____
_____
_____
_____
_____
_____
_____
_____
_____
_____
_____
_____
_____

# MARCH 13

## HASTY

**Q:** When I take tests at school, I have a problem. I always like being the first one done. It makes me feel good that I'm already done, and everyone else is struggling to finish. The problem is that I never check my work, so I make a lot of dumb mistakes and get Ds and Fs on my tests. It's not that I don't know the subject; I just don't check my work. When I don't finish a test first, I usually get a better grade, but I feel stupid being one of the last kids to finish. I want good grades, but I don't know how to get rid of this feeling of having to finish first all the time.

**What God Says:** Proverbs 19:2 *Zeal without knowledge is not good; a person who moves too quickly may go the wrong way.*[*]

**A:** There is an old expression: Haste makes waste. When you do things too fast, you are bound to make mistakes. Finishing first is just to boost your ego in a race that really means nothing whatsoever. You sound like an intelligent person, so do as God says. Slow down and stop trying to finish so quickly. Going the fast way in life may mean that you will be making dumb mistakes throughout your life.

## Questions to ponder:

Do you try to do things too quickly?
Why or why not?

Life's a journey. Don't be so hasty.

**JOURNAL:**_____

_____
_____
_____
_____
_____
_____
_____
_____
_____
_____
_____
_____
_____
_____
_____
_____
_____
_____
_____
_____
_____

# LONELINESS

**Q:** My cheerleading friends at school are all nice and cool. We hang out a lot at school and after games and sometimes on weekends. One day, one of my cheerleading friends found out I was going to church on Sundays and youth group on Sunday nights. Once the word spread, it seemed that those friends didn't want to hang out with me anymore. They started ignoring me at school and stopped inviting me over to their houses on weekends. During games, they talked among themselves and didn't include me. I felt isolated like I had a disease. It made me extremely sad and lonely, and I don't know what to do.

> **What God Says:** 1 Peter 4:19 *If you are suffering according to God's will, keep on doing what is right and trust yourself to God who made you, for He will never fail you.**

**A:** Sometimes, we feel alone in our stand for Christ. We can take comfort in knowing that there are many people who are equally as committed to God as we are, and He will reward that commitment. Stand strong in your faith and don't be discouraged, for God is with you and watching out for you. He will comfort your loneliness. And with God on your side, you really are never alone.

**Questions to ponder:**
How often do you get lonely?
How do you get over your loneliness?

> If you feel lonely for God's sake,
> you are truly blessed.

**JOURNAL:**_____

_____

_____

_____

_____

_____

_____

_____

_____

_____

_____

_____

_____

_____

_____

_____

_____

_____

_____

_____

_____

_____

_____

# MARCH 15

## DEALING WITH HOT-TEMPERED PEOPLE

**Q:** My parents got a divorce about two years ago. My step-dad has a terrible temper. When he gets mad, he likes to yell a lot for a long period of time. When he is really angry, he will throw things like glasses or the TV remote or whatever is nearby. His anger usually lasts about an hour, and then everything calms down. He usually apologizes afterward, but his hot temper scares me to death. Sometimes, I think he might throw something at me and hurt me real bad. I don't know what to do when he gets in those rages.

> **What God Says:** Proverbs 29:22 *A hot-tempered person starts fights and gets into all kinds of sin.*\*

**A:** If you look at Jesus's life, it is totally opposite of how your stepdad acts. Jesus is gentle, loving, and kind-hearted, welcoming children to him. Your stepdad is arrogant, violent, and scary to children. If your mom can't control his actions, you could consider living with your dad or a grandparent. No person should have to live in fear of a hot-tempered person. As God says, a hot-tempered person is full of sin and not someone we want to live with. But first, pray to God to give you strength and wisdom to do the right thing.

### Question to ponder:

How do you deal with hot-tempered people?

A hot temper is a stepping-stone to worse sin.

**JOURNAL:**

# MARCH 16

**Q:** I won't play with any of the white boys in my sixth-grade class—not because they are mean or unfriendly, but because they are white. See, my dad works at a factory, and his boss is a white man who is always being mean to my dad, making him do things that none of the white workers have to do. My dad told me that white people don't like black people, so I shouldn't get involved with them at school. Sometimes, I'm real mean to some of the white kids for no reason just to get even for what my dad puts up with every day. If white men are mean to him at work, then I'll be mean to white kids at school.

> **What God Says:** Ephesians 2:14 *Christ himself has made peace between Jews and you Gentiles by making all one people. He has broken down the wall of hostility that used to separate us.*\*

**A:** Christ died to destroy all barriers of hostility that sin has created between people. How the boss treats your dad is wrong, and your dad should report this person to higher authorities to get him fired. However, that doesn't give you the right to treat the kids at school just as badly. Your sin against those white boys at school does not make up for the sin your father is enduring at work. All people—white, black, Asian, Indian, whatever—are equal in God's eyes. Start treating all your classmates with love and respect, and tear down those walls of racism.

### Questions to ponder:

What is your opinion of racism?

Is there racism in your school?

Explain.

Following Christ means you are color-blind.

**JOURNAL:** _____

_____
_____
_____
_____
_____
_____
_____
_____
_____
_____
_____
_____
_____
_____
_____
_____
_____
_____
_____
_____
_____
_____
_____

# NOSY PARENTS

**Q:** I don't have any privacy at home whatsoever. My mom is always listening to my phone calls. She reads my notes between me and my friends. I have to keep my bedroom door open all the time, even when I'm dressing. She goes through my closets and dresser drawers all the time. I don't know why she does that because I've never done anything that would make her not trust me. When I confront her about her nosiness, she just says, "I was 13 years old once. I know what they do." I can't keep living in my house with someone who is constantly in my business.

> **What God Says:** 1 Peter 4:15 *"If you suffer, however, it must not be for murder, stealing, making trouble, or prying into other people's affairs."*

**A:** Do you see how God puts "prying into other people's affairs" in the same category as murderers and thieves? That shows how God feels about people who are nosy for no reason. Talk to your dad and see if he can help. Or talk to your grandparents on your mom's side to find out why your mom is so distrusting (or overprotective) of you. The more information you can get, the better chance you will have to fix this situation. Respectfully, show her the passage above, and lovingly tell her how sad you feel that she doesn't trust you.

**Questions to ponder:**
Why do you think some parents are nosy?
Do you think it's wrong? Why or why not?

Nosy people are not welcome in God's eyes.

**JOURNAL:** _____

_____

_____

_____

_____

_____

_____

_____

_____

_____

_____

_____

_____

_____

_____

_____

_____

_____

_____

_____

_____

_____

_____

# MARCH 18

## RETALIATION

**Q:** I was shopping at the mall the other day, and this girl I knew from another school stole my purse. I put my purse down to try on a sweater, and she just took it and ran out of the store, laughing. I had everything in my purse, including my personal diary with many private things in it. She started spreading stories to all her friends about what I had written in my diary, just to make me look bad. So, here is what I'm going to do. I know she likes this guy at my school, so I'm going to spread a rumor that she's easy and loose and that she has kissed many boys, just so her reputation will be ruined. Then, she'll be too embarrassed to go out with this guy.

> **What God Says:** 1 Peter 3:9 *Don't repay evil for evil. Don't retaliate when people say unkind things about you. Instead, pay them back with a blessing. That is what God wants you to do, and He will bless you for it.\**

**A:** Learning to love our enemies and not repay evil for evil is one of the hardest things God asks us to do. It's especially hard when someone intentionally hurts us. You need to think about the life of Christ. People mocked Him, spit on Him, and judged Him unfairly when He did absolutely nothing wrong. He could have easily retaliated, but He forgave them. I know we are only humans and not Jesus, but we can try to be like Him, and we will truly be blessed if we do.

### Question to ponder:

Have you ever retaliated or wanted to retaliate against someone? Explain the situation and what you did.

Forgive your enemies; don't retaliate.

**JOURNAL:**

# MARCH 19

## HELPING A SUFFERING FRIEND

**Q:** I really want to help my friend across the street. She is going through a difficult time. First, her mom died about a year ago from lung cancer, and her grandmother passed away last month. She was really close to both of them, and the news of each death just devastated her. Then, after all this, her brother tried to commit suicide by slicing his throat. He will live, but he's in the hospital and may never talk again. And through all this, her dad started drinking very heavily and staying out late, leaving my friend and her little sister home alone. She is going through a lot, and I don't know how to help her.

**What God Says:** 2 Corinthians 1:3–4 *All praise to the God and father of our Lord Jesus Christ. He is the source of every mercy and the God who comforts us. He comforts us in all our troubles so that we can comfort others. When others are troubled, we will be able to give them the same comfort God has given us.\**

**A:** WOW! What a difficult year for your friend. She has been hit by tragedy after tragedy in her young life. But as the passage says, we can offer comfort just as God has comforted us during our time of need. You just need to be a good friend, spending time with her and helping her with anything at her house. Remember to tell her that God will never give us more than we can handle and that He loves her. Pray for her, and be her comforting friend.

### Question to ponder:
How do you deal with a suffering friend?
Give examples from your life.

God comforts a suffering friend.

**JOURNAL:**

_____

_____

_____

_____

_____

_____

_____

_____

_____

_____

_____

_____

_____

_____

_____

_____

_____

_____

_____

_____

_____

_____

# YOU LIKE SOMEONE, BUT YOUR FRIENDS DON'T

**Q:** There is a boy I really like in the eighth grade. I've known him since the fourth grade, and he is really nice and friendly. The problem is that my friends think he's a geek. That's only because he doesn't wear cool clothes and sometimes acts dumb in a funny sort of way. But I really like him a lot. My friends are always teasing me and giving me a hard time about him. They won't allow him to hang with us at school. They don't even try to get to know him. They'd rather just laugh at him and not give him a chance. How can I keep my friends and yet still like this boy?

> **What God Says:** John 7:24 "Look beneath the surface so you can judge correctly."

**A:** God is very specific about judging others by their outward appearance. If you judge others, then you too will be judged. What you need to do is help your friends get to know this boy on a smaller scale, maybe one or two friends at a time. Kids have a tendency to want to be cool in front of a larger group but to be more approachable in a smaller group. Let them find out what a nice person this boy is and go from there. Then, after they find out what a decent person he is, tell your friends what John 7:24 says so they won't judge wrongly in the future.

**Questions to ponder:**
Have you ever liked a person that your friends didn't?
If so, how did you handle it?
If not, how would you handle it?

Don't judge someone by his or her appearance.

**JOURNAL:**

_____

_____

_____

_____

_____

_____

_____

_____

_____

_____

_____

_____

_____

_____

_____

_____

_____

_____

_____

_____

_____

_____

_____

# MARCH 21

## APPEARANCE-CONSCIOUS

**Q:** I go to a school in a richer part of town. My parents separated, so I am living with my grandparents. This is the school I have to go to in the district. The kids are pretty nice, but they are so materialistic and appearance-conscious. They all must wear the right brand of clothes and the cool shoes that cost five times more than what I can afford. I can only afford clearance-type clothes and secondhand shoes, and it seems like people are always pointing at me and giggling behind my back. I try not to pay attention, but it's tough when people are judging you like that. What can I do?

> **What God Says:** 1 Peter 3:3–4 *Don't be concerned about the outward beauty that depends on fancy hairstyles, expensive jewelry, or beautiful clothes. You should be known for the beauty that comes from within, the unfading beauty of a gentle and quiet spirit so precious to God.*\*

**A:** It's difficult when you don't fit in with the crowd at your age because you can't afford the expensive clothes or brand-name shoes. But no one can take away your loving heart or your kind spirit that means more to God than any expensive item. You will have days that are frustrating and discouraging, but pray to God to give you strength and perseverance to not change your heart. Resist the devil's attempt to change you to an appearance-conscious person.

### Questions to ponder:
How appearance-conscious is your school?

Is it a problem for you personally?

God notices the beauty of the heart.

**JOURNAL:**

# MARCH 22

## DEALING WITH CONSTANT COMPLAINERS

**Q:** I have a friend at school who is always complaining about something. He complains a lot about his parents making him do chores, or he complains about his teachers giving too much homework. He complains about his older and younger brothers being brats and mean to him. He even complains about the other kids in the class, especially at lunch when he loses a game. He's a nice guy, but I get tired of the constant complaining. What can I do to get him to stop?

> **What God Says:** Philippians 2:14–15 *In everything you do, stay away from complaining and arguing so no one can speak a word of blame against you. You are to live clean, innocent lives as children of God in a dark world full of crooked and perverse people. Let your lives shine brightly before them.\**

**A:** All complaining does is bring people down. It does nothing to uplift the spirits of those around you. Talk to your friend and ask him in a positive way to stop complaining about life and start appreciating those things that God has provided for him in his life. Also, if you are always positive with him, your shining light might get his attention so he will change his ways. People seem to adapt to the people around them, so the more upbeat and positive you are, the better chance that he will stop complaining about everything.

### Questions to ponder:
Why do kids complain so much?

How often do you complain?

Always complaining is just a waste of breath.

**JOURNAL:** _____

_____
_____
_____
_____
_____
_____
_____
_____
_____
_____
_____
_____
_____
_____
_____
_____
_____
_____
_____
_____
_____
_____

# FEARS

**Q:** I have a lot of fears. If there is a phobia, then I probably have it. I am deathly afraid of heights. Believe it or not, I could not have a bedroom on the second floor for fear of looking out my window. I have fears of small places ever since my evil grandfather locked me in a closet for almost 24 hours when I was very young because I was crying too much. I also have a problem being around a lot of people at a mall or a concert. I always feel that people are staring at me and judging me. I'm only 14 years old, but I have a lot of fears. I have tried to get over my fears, but when I get in an uncomfortable situation, my fears come back. Is there any hope for me?

---

**What God Says:** Joshua 1:9 *"Be strong and courageous! Do not be afraid or discouraged. For the LORD your God is with you wherever you go."*

---

**A:** The types of fears you are describing are mostly in your mind. Sometimes, you can control your fear if you can control your mind, but it takes God for this to be accomplished. God can provide you the strength and courage to face your fears and conquer them in your mind. It's mind over matter. If you can convince yourself that heights, small rooms, or crowds will not hurt you, you can conquer your fears. And there is a great peace in knowing that God will be with you every step of the way to encourage and support you. Make a decision today to conquer your fears and allow God to help you in this quest.

## Questions to ponder:

What are your biggest fears?
How do you deal with them?

When you fully trust God, your fears go away.

**JOURNAL:** _____

_____

_____

_____

_____

_____

_____

_____

_____

_____

_____

_____

_____

_____

_____

_____

_____

_____

_____

_____

_____

_____

# MARCH 24

## DEALING WITH KIDS WITH HYGIENE PROBLEMS

**Q:** There is a girl in my school who has bad hygiene problems. She does not shave her legs (she's 13 years old), yet she wears shorts to school. She rarely brushes her hair and probably only washes it once a week. Sometimes, I can tell that she didn't put on deodorant because she smells funny. Most of the kids at school just laugh at her or ignore her, but she's a sweet kid, and I would like to help her. I don't know much about her family except that she has no mom and her dad works a lot. How can I help her?

> **What God Says:** 2 Timothy 2:21 *If you keep yourself pure, you will be a utensil God can use for His purpose. Your life will be clean, and you will be ready for the master to use you for every good work.*\*

**A:** Read the verse above again. You are right to be concerned about this girl at your school. Although God does not care about our outer appearance, we must be clean both inside and out to be ready to do God's work. We need to keep our hearts pure on the inside and our bodies clean on the outside. The solution may seem a little confusing, but it really isn't. As representatives of Christ, how we present ourselves is important in both looks and actions. See, if our body odor or unclean outer appearance is a distraction from people hearing God's word, then our works are useless. It seems like your friend needs a female touch since she has no female influence at her house. Invite her over and show her how to take care of herself, and make herself presentable. She may not know what is so obvious to you.

### Questions to ponder:

Do you know of kids who have hygiene problems?

How could you help them?

> You can't do God's work
> if your appearance is a distraction.

**JOURNAL:** _____

_____

_____

_____

_____

_____

_____

_____

_____

_____

_____

_____

_____

_____

_____

_____

_____

_____

_____

_____

# MARCH 25

## MATURITY

**Q:** I am an 11-year-old girl who is very mature for my age. I could easily pass for 14 or 15 years old. When I wear makeup, I could pass for 16. I've had 15- or 16-year-old guys ask me out. I want to go out with them because they are so cute and mature, but my parents won't let me. I'm mature enough to know the dangers of dating, and I can look after myself. But my parents are afraid that I'm growing up too fast, which could get me into trouble. I really want to date and go to teen clubs, but my parents are so conservative.

> **What God Says:** Isaiah 26:7 *But for those who are righteous, your path is not steep or rough. You are a God of justice, and you smooth out the road ahead of them.**

**A:** You may think you are mature enough to handle dating and clubs, but I'm not sure that's the best thing for an 11-year-old girl. God says to allow Him to guide you down the right path. You might be very mature at 11, but you lack the emotional experience in dealing with the issues that teenagers go through. Don't try to grow up too fast. You'll get there faster than you think. Enjoy your youth for as long as you have it, and always ask God for guidance along the way.

## Question to ponder:

What is your opinion of the old saying, "You are growing up too fast"?

Don't try to grow up too fast.

**JOURNAL:**

_____

_____
_____
_____
_____
_____
_____
_____
_____
_____
_____
_____
_____
_____
_____
_____
_____
_____
_____
_____
_____

# MARCH 26

**Q:** I love to ride my bike. When I get home from school, I immediately jump on my bike and meet my friends at this big dirt field where we ride and jump and do tricks in the dirt. The other day, I had a ton of homework, from a test to a worksheet plus a book report, all due the next day. But I decided to go ride my bicycle first before starting my homework. Well, I got home after dark, and after eating dinner and cleaning up, I had little time to get this homework done. Consequently, I failed my test and got an incomplete on my book report. Now, I may not graduate from the eighth grade until I complete these assignments.

> **What God Says:** 1 Samuel 14:36 *Then Saul said, "Let's chase the Philistines all night and destroy every last one of them." His men replied, "We'll do whatever you think is best." But the priest said, "Let's ask God first."*\*

**A:** Setting the right priorities means being responsible. Play and fun must take a back seat to homework and chores. But when there's a conflict in priorities, you need to seek God and ask Him for help, and He will guide you down the right path in the proper way. Read the verse above. Notice that every time there was a decision to be made about battles, the Israelite priest asked the Lord for guidance. When he did this, the Israelites were victorious. When he failed to ask God, the enemy slaughtered the Israelites. So remember, His way is always the right way, and He will set your priorities in the right direction.

## Questions to ponder:

How do you handle multiple priorities?

How do you manage your time?

Let God lead your life.

**JOURNAL:**

_____

_____

_____

_____

_____

_____

_____

_____

_____

_____

_____

_____

_____

_____

_____

_____

_____

_____

_____

_____

_____

_____

_____

# HELPING FRIENDS WITH LUSTFUL THOUGHTS

**Q:** My friend can't get this seventh-grade girl out of his mind. My friend is in the eighth grade, and he really likes this girl. She looks much older than her age, and she is extremely well-endowed. He describes his thoughts to me about this girl, how she probably looks in a bikini and other lustful ideas. The girl is on his mind 24/7, and it's beginning to affect his schoolwork, his home life, and even his friendship with me. I need him to start thinking about other things like school and skating and to stop thinking about her body.

**What God Says:** Philippians 4:8 *Think about things that are pure and lovely and admirable.**

**A:** When we fill our minds with purity and goodness, then lust has no place to dwell. It sounds like your friend has very active hormones. That is fairly natural for boys that age. The key is to keep these lustful thoughts to a minimum and focus on other things that are more important, like God. Get your friend involved in other activities with other boys and talk to him about God. The more active you are, the less time there is to have lustful thoughts.

**Questions to ponder:**

Why in your opinion are lustful thoughts bad?

How can you help kids deal with constant lustful thoughts?

Out-of-control lust leads to mightier sins.

**JOURNAL:**
_____

_____
_____
_____
_____
_____
_____
_____
_____
_____
_____
_____
_____
_____
_____
_____
_____
_____
_____
_____
_____
_____

## LACK OF CONFIDENCE

**Q:** Many people have told me that I have a beautiful singing voice. I love to sing in front of the mirror at home and even in front of my family. I sometimes sing with my friends when we are just messing around. The problem is that I can't sing in front of strangers. When asked to sing in front of the entire church, I got so scared that I declined. When I went to a karaoke place with my family and was asked to sing at the front of the restaurant, I couldn't do it. I just don't have the confidence to sing in front of strangers.

> **What God Says:** Proverbs 3:26 *"For the LORD is your security. He will keep your foot from being caught in the trap."*

**A:** Lean on God when your confidence is low, and He will strengthen you. It doesn't matter if everyone tells you how good you are. If you don't believe it, you won't feel confident. But God is the great comforter, and if you ask Him for support, amazing things will happen. Overcoming this fear may lead you down the road to a successful singing career.

**Questions to ponder:**

What do you do when your confidence is low?

Explain a situation when your confidence was low and what you did.

God is your solution for a confidence booster.

**JOURNAL:**_____

_____

_____

_____

_____

_____

_____

_____

_____

_____

_____

_____

_____

_____

_____

_____

_____

_____

_____

_____

_____

_____

# HELPING IRRESPONSIBLE KIDS

**Q:** I have a good friend who is totally irresponsible. He is constantly losing things such as his books and calculator or his pencils and pens. He is constantly borrowing things from me and never returning them because he loses them. Also, I would say that four out of five nights, he has to call me up because he forgot his homework assignment sheet, forgot his book, or lost his school worksheet. He's not dumb. He just doesn't think about things. It's getting pretty annoying, and I'd like to know how to help him become more responsible.

> **What God Says:** Matthew 25:20–21 *The servant said, "Sir, you gave me five bags of gold to invest, and I have doubled the amount." The master was full of praise. "Well done, my good and faithful servant. You have been faithful in handling this small amount, so now I will give you many more responsibilities. Let's celebrate together!"\**

**A:** God will bless those with more treasures if they are responsible with the ones they already have. To become responsible, your friend needs to focus on his responsibilities. The easiest way to do that is to have him write everything down that he needs and read it before he leaves school or home. By keeping a planner, it will keep him more focused and responsible. God expects his children to be responsible.

**Question to ponder:**

How do you help irresponsible kids?

Change your habits and become more responsible.

**JOURNAL:**

## STRESS

**Q:** I have a major problem taking tests. I study hard and usually know the material, but when I take a test, I am so nervous that I cannot think clearly. All of a sudden, my mind goes blank, and I don't do well on the test. My parents and teachers think it's stress. I stress so much when I take a test that I can't think. I'm in the eighth grade now, and I know that when I get to high school, it will get much worse. I need to solve this stress problem now, but where do I start?

> **What God Says:** Psalm 119:143 *"As pressures and stress bear down on me, I find joy in your commands."*

**A:** Stress is caused in the mind, and it's a by-product of worry. If you know the material and study hard, that's when you need to put all your books away and concentrate on something else. The key to reducing stress is relaxation and calmness, and God provides both of those in His word. So read God's word to relax and unwind, and when you take tests, take a deep breath and relax. Then say a short prayer to guide you on the test, and go for it!

## Questions to ponder:
How do you handle stress?
What do you do when you feel stressed?

God's word is the best medicine
to calm stress.

**JOURNAL:** _____

_____

_____

_____

_____

_____

_____

_____

_____

_____

_____

_____

_____

_____

_____

_____

_____

_____

_____

_____

_____

## DEALING WITH VIOLENT KIDS

**Q:** There is a kid in school whom nobody likes because he is so violent toward the smaller kids. One of the girls in my class is a friend of mine. She was walking home from school one day when this kid snuck up behind her and pushed her down very hard. There was no reason. He wasn't with anyone, so he wasn't trying to impress anybody. He just pushed her down and started laughing as he raced down the street on his skateboard. My friend scraped her knee and sprained her wrist, and now she's afraid to walk home alone for fear that this violent kid will do it to her again.

**What God Says**: Psalm 12:5 *"The LORD replies, 'I have seen violence done to the helpless, and I have heard the groans of the poor. Now I will rise up to rescue them, as they have longed for me to do.'"*

**A:** To put it simply, God hates all violence, and He hates the violence kids do toward innocent people. God has promised to surely judge the violent severely. Somehow, this bully needs to be put in his place. You may need to find someone bigger than he is to talk with (or slightly intimidate) him and put some sense into him. He needs to stop harassing younger, more vulnerable kids. Maybe, when he sees the effects of his actions, he will stop. Always remember that God will protect the helpless and innocent, and He hears their prayers.

**Questions to ponder:**

Why do kids do violent things to innocent kids?

Do you know kids like this?

Explain.

God's wrath will always prevail
against the enemy.

**JOURNAL:**

_____

_____

_____

_____

_____

_____

_____

_____

_____

_____

_____

_____

_____

_____

_____

_____

_____

_____

_____

_____

**The life lessons I have learned this month are:**

_____

_____

_____

_____

_____

_____

_____

_____

_____

_____

_____

_____

_____

_____

_____

_____

_____

_____

_____

_____

_____

_____

_____

# APPENDIX 1: CATEGORIES LISTED ALPHABETICALLY

| Month | Day | Category |
|---|---|---|
| February | 7 | Accountability |
| March | 2 | Acting before you think |
| January | 17 | Anger |
| January | 30 | Anxiety |
| March | 21 | Appearance-conscious |
| January | 2 | Attitude |
| February | 21 | Bad habits |
| January | 5 | Bad influences |
| March | 10 | Baptism |
| January | 27 | Belonging |
| January | 19 | Blaming |
| February | 12 | Choices |
| February | 24 | Cocky kids |
| February | 9 | Comparing one kid to another |
| March | 4 | Conforming to wrong |
| March | 22 | Constant complainers |
| February | 16 | Criticizing |
| March | 7 | Cussing |
| February | 28 | Dating |
| February | 25 | Decision-making |
| March | 6 | Discipline |
| March | 12 | Discouraged |
| January | 6 | Disrespectful kids |

| | | |
|---|---|---|
| January | 9 | Modesty |
| January | 18 | Never satisfied |
| March | 17 | Nosy parents |
| January | 7 | Peer pressure |
| February | 26 | Prayers not answered |
| January | 22 | Prejudiced people |
| March | 26 | Priorities |
| March | 16 | Racism |
| February | 3 | Rejection |
| March | 18 | Retaliation |
| February | 4 | Revenge |
| February | 23 | Salvation questions |
| January | 3 | Self-control |
| January | 12 | Selfish kids |
| January | 25 | Shyness |
| March | 5 | Sibling rivalry |
| January | 23 | Stealing |
| March | 30 | Stress |
| February | 18 | Strict parents |
| January | 15 | Suffering |
| January | 31 | Teacher problems |
| January | 29 | Temptation |
| February | 19 | Trials |
| February | 10 | Truth about the Bible |
| February | 15 | Unpopular kids |
| January | 16 | Unreliable friends |
| March | 3 | Unworthy of God |
| January | 10 | Vain kids |
| March | 31 | Violent kids |
| March | 11 | Watching too much TV |
| February | 5 | Witnessing |
| January | 24 | Worry |
| March | 20 | You like someone, but your friends don't |

# APPENDIX 2: THOUGHTS FOR THE DAY

| Month | Day | Thought for the Day |
|-------|-----|---------------------|
| January | 1 | God will never leave you. |
| January | 2 | Work for God with a cheerful heart. |
| January | 3 | Let God control your temper. |
| January | 4 | God always has perfect timing. |
| January | 5 | A good tree will yield good fruit. |
| January | 6 | Always respect your elders. |
| January | 7 | Don't let peer pressure destroy your good character. |
| January | 8 | Trust God to help you change from your sinful ways. |
| January | 9 | Be modest, and people will respect you more. |
| January | 10 | Inward beauty is more important than outward appearance. |
| January | 11 | Let God's will be done in your life. |
| January | 12 | God loves an unselfish heart. |
| January | 13 | Heaven waits for those who know Christ. |
| January | 14 | Turn first to God in times of fear. |
| January | 15 | Jesus says blessed are those persecuted for my sake. |
| January | 16 | God can make an unreliable soul truly reliable. |
| January | 17 | God says to think before you talk. |
| January | 18 | God satisfies all our needs. |
| January | 19 | When you are wrongfully blamed, seek God. |
| January | 20 | God has a place in heaven for those who follow Him. |
| January | 21 | Never be embarrassed about your love for God. |
| January | 22 | Fight the terrible sin of prejudice. |
| January | 23 | Thieves are not allowed in the kingdom of God unless they repent. |

January  24  Cast all your worries on God.
January  25  God is with us always.
January  26  Ignorance is a sin we must avoid.
January  27  Belong to the right group: Followers of Jesus Christ.
January  28  God is love. There is no room in a person's heart for hate.
January  29  God, lead us not into temptation.
January  30  Cast all your anxieties on the Lord.
January  31  Respect your authorities.
February  1  Turn to God for forgiveness.
February  2  Keep up with your responsibilities before they become a crisis.
February  3  God will heal a rejected/dejected heart.
February  4  God will take care of the wicked in His way.
February  5  God calls all of us to be witnesses to His word.
February  6  Focus on God, for He will lead you down the right path.
February  7  We are all accountable to God for our deeds.
February  8  Without faith in God, we have nothing.
February  9  Never judge others unfairly lest you be judged.
February 10  The Bible is the source of God's word.
February 11  Parents are expected to care for and love their children.
February 12  Make the right choice. Live for God.
February 13  Use your talents to glorify God.
February 14  Grumbling is a useless sin.
February 15  Let God take care of your enemies.
February 16  Unnecessary criticism leads to hardships.
February 17  Lean on God when dealing with fear.
February 18  Always use discipline in a godly manner.
February 19  Make sure you are innocent in your trials with God.
February 20  Don't forget about God's children, or God may forget about you.
February 21  Bad habits are hard to break. Ask God for help.
February 22  You can't take your things to heaven.
February 23  No one can come to the father except through Jesus.
February 24  Cockiness will not get you into the kingdom of God.
February 25  Trust God with your difficult decisions.
February 26  Never give up on God.

| | | |
|---|---|---|
| February | 27 | God hates all evil. |
| February | 28 | Use good judgment before dating. |
| March | 1 | God cannot tolerate a lying tongue. |
| March | 2 | Always think before you act. |
| March | 3 | Thank you, Lord, for sending your son. |
| March | 4 | We need to conform our minds and hearts to doing what is good. |
| March | 5 | God never compares one child to another. |
| March | 6 | Godly discipline is a necessary part of life. |
| March | 7 | The tongue can be mightier than the sword. |
| March | 8 | Bad lyrics could lead to bad behavior. |
| March | 9 | There is no doubt that God exists. |
| March | 10 | Baptism solidifies your faith in Christ. |
| March | 11 | Don't be an idle Christian. |
| March | 12 | Don't be discouraged for doing the right thing. |
| March | 13 | Life's a journey. Don't be so hasty. |
| March | 14 | If you feel lonely for God's sake, you are truly blessed. |
| March | 15 | A hot temper is a stepping-stone to worse sin. |
| March | 16 | Following Christ means you are color-blind. |
| March | 17 | Nosy people are not welcome in God's eyes. |
| March | 18 | Forgive your enemies; don't retaliate. |
| March | 19 | God comforts a suffering friend. |
| March | 20 | Don't judge someone by his or her appearance. |
| March | 21 | God notices the beauty of the heart. |
| March | 22 | Always complaining is just a waste of breath. |
| March | 23 | When you fully trust God, your fears go away. |
| March | 24 | You can't do God's work if your appearance is a distraction. |
| March | 25 | Don't try to grow up too fast. |
| March | 26 | Let God lead your life. |
| March | 27 | Out-of-control lust leads to mightier sins. |
| March | 28 | God is your solution for a confidence booster. |
| March | 29 | Change your habits and become more responsible. |
| March | 30 | God's word is the best medicine to calm stress. |
| March | 31 | God's wrath will always prevail against the enemy. |

www.ingramcontent.com/pod-product-compliance
Lightning Source LLC
Chambersburg PA
CBHW071430090426
42737CB00011B/1615